SURVIVING
CHAOS

HOW I FOUND PEACE
AT A BEACH BAR

HAROLD PHIFER

Edited by Author Connections, LLC
Cover design by 1106 Design

This book is a memoir, based on real events.

TITLE: Surviving Chaos: How I Found Peace at a Beach Bar

ISBN: 978-0-578-74353-0 (E-Book)
ISBN: 978-0-578-74354-7 (Paperback)

Library of Congress Catalog Card Number: 2020914975

1st Edition

For information, email info@risepubbooks.com

Table of Contents

Introduction

I grew up in a severely dysfunctional environment where I was constantly manipulated by my controlling aunt, abused by my mindless big brother, and shamed by my schizophrenic mom. Ducking, dodging, and going un-noticed were daily rituals.

The most troubling of all was my mother's relationship with The Walls. It took a near-death experience from a terrorist attack in Afghanistan to force me to deal with issues I tried to hide for fifty-plus years. Throughout this story and in my life, I use humor to sustain me, because logic didn't apply.

After living in Afghanistan for ten years, I can say with certainty that only the fools, the desperate, and the greedy dare to return to that unstable place. Unfortunately, I fall into one or more of those categories.

My story touches on the sad, the shocking, and the schizophrenic behaviors that surrounded me until well into adulthood. You will meet both male and female bullies. You will get a raw peek into what it's like to be raised by a mentally ill mother and a greedy, calculating aunt.

My childhood and my career contained chaotic events. Once the characters are established, you will find these two segments comically meshed throughout many of those abnormal circumstances.

This journey opens in the tropical Southeast Asian country of Thailand, where I took refuge after the blast in Afghanistan. I was living a carefree life with no worries or drama. By happenstance, I came across another lost soul. He was hiding from life, just like me. Dylan took advantage of my drunken state and easily coerced me into divulging my life's history. He opened a door that led us both on a whirlwind tour neither of us expected or imagined. Many of these stories may stick with you like nothing you have ever experienced, read, or heard before.

Wagon Wheel on the Beach

On a lazy Sunday afternoon in Thailand, I wasn't doing much more than watching bikini-clad beauty queens on the beach. Since arriving in that tropical paradise, my days have been filled with kicking seashells in the sand, skipping rocks into the ocean, counting the dolphins that leapt into the air, and drinking. My go-to ritual was three margaritas to start. Then, my evenings unfolded in a blur, with a smile.

There was nothing in this new world remotely close to what I'd left behind. I wasn't thinking much about my past. I wasn't thinking at all. I was overjoyed to allow my brain a rest.

Out of nowhere, an older gentleman approached me on the beach. He'd missed his window for a massage, just as I had. Most of the time, I was undisturbed and spoiled in my solitude, so initially I resented the intrusion. This man was in his early seventies, stood about six feet tall, and was slightly overweight with long, salty hair. I could tell he was a free spirit by his disheveled island appearance and the half-liter drinking mug he carried. I wasn't quite feeling any vibe of a surfer wannabe.

The man had been watching me for days as I policed the sand and coached the crabs back into the sea. I was keenly aware of his presence but could not fathom why he was so interested and paying attention to me. It was pretty obvious that we were from starkly different worlds. He gave off an air of leisure and luxury, which didn't suit my own energy of escapism in self preservation. Yes, we were from the same country, but without speaking a word to each other it was clear we were total opposites. Living abroad creates a new perspective, but your roots are forever. For reasons I can't explain, I held our differences against him.

Without sensing my disdain, the man boldly walked over to ask where I was from and what brought me to this lovely country. Not wanting to spill my beans to a stranger, I flipped the inquiry on the nosy white guy.

"What brought YOU here?" I asked.

He was eager to talk. His name was Dylan, and he was from New York. A retired banker living abroad. It was clear from his appearance that paradise had taken a toll on this American. Thailand had him in the mix of never-ending parties, sightseeing, and an endless stream of level-ten cuties; the very reasons I had been drawn to the place as well.

It wasn't hard to understand that Dylan saw me as a badly needed friend. However, I was certain that I didn't need anything. As for friends, I had none. Even my own dog had betrayed me. When I took him for a walk, he used our outing as an opportunity to flee. So, Thailand was my new comrade and cover. It was a blanket like no other. If I had been called home for any reason at that time, I would have yelled out, "Good Lord, let Thailand be my exit gate!"

Dylan was a divorcee, like me. His kids were successful adults, like their dad. He was oozing with pride over his bio, but I was beaming too. My kids are unique achievers. Dylan went on to say that he was in Thailand for a new lease on life. The land of sun, surf, and sand was his fresh start.

He must have noticed that I was distracted by the g-stringed girls on the beach; he asked once more how I'd gotten there. Begrudgingly, I turned toward him and said, "Dylan, my life has been in stages; like the spokes of a wagon wheel. Each spoke may carry the same weight, but they make up the highs and lows of my existence."

Dylan grinned in response. Perhaps he sensed a gut-wrenching story from a fellow drunkard. "Continue on, my friend."

I wasn't pleased that he had called me his friend, but the morning's margaritas had worked their magic. I'd already consumed more than my starter pack; something had to give. I could get up and stagger away, or I could give Dylan an earful of the sad stories that glued me together. I began to unload.

"Until 2009, my life was a constant push and shove from day to day. Some things were my fault, but I'd been dealt a string of bad hands. People have always tried to box me in. Even when things appeared above board, there was always a hidden catch. Leaving the U.S. was my way of escaping that loop.

"Ten years ago, I took my career to the international level. The decision was about more than money. It seemed a good way to flee the pain and humiliation of losing my kids, my finances, and my self-respect. I thought, *What the hell? What more do I have to lose?* So I accepted an independent contractor position in Afghanistan, which is where I nearly lost my life."

Dylan's eyes were wide. He asked what happened to me over there.

"As you may have read or heard, roadside bombs and suicide attacks happen year round in Afghanistan. I wasn't ignorant to the possibility of being blown to shreds, but being in the middle of such an attack gave me a mental rewind I wasn't prepared for. Somehow, I survived the biggest explosion to ever hit that war-torn country."

The man placed his hand over his mouth. In a low, conspiring tone, he said, "We have nothing but crabs, turtles, seagulls, and pelicans as our audience. If you care to, please go on."

I glared at him and thought, *This guy must be a glutton for some crazy, crazy crap. Well, I have plenty of it!*

I said to Dylan, "If you want to buy the drinks, I'll do the talking."

I had been feasting on that heavenly beach, soaked in booze for months on end. Why not peel back the pages? If this burned-out banker from New York was willing to fund my stupor, what was the harm in unloading the demons?

Without a second thought, Dylan shot back, "You have a deal, my man." With a wide grin, he reached his hand out and shook mine. "The drinks are on me. I want to hear about every spoke in your wagon wheel."

PART I:
BLAST TO THE PAST

Tick, Tick, BOOM!

The day the bomb hit, I'd had a strange feeling that something was amiss, but couldn't put my finger on it. I kept staring at the guards, the cleaners, and the cooks, trying to find a clue as to what was making me so antsy.

Around 3:00 p.m., I returned to the barracks from work. I wanted to take a nap but couldn't sleep, and I couldn't understand my restlessness. Instead, I took a quiet walk around camp to settle my nerves. After my short surveillance, I returned to my room to lie down, then woke up in time for dinner at 6:00 p.m. It was winter and daylight turned in early.

In the cafeteria, I saw Mike, Ace, and Jackson sitting close to the door. Suddenly, there was a rumble, enough to cause a panic, followed by a massive blast. This was no earthquake. It felt more like a rendition of The Big Bang.

The entire building levitated for a few seconds, then slammed violently to the ground. As the place went black I knew I was at the doorsteps of death. Everyone in the cafeteria was covered in glass, asbestos, and wall plaster. Jackson and I were thrown about twenty feet across the room, and landed next to a counter. We scurried behind it. Jackson appeared ghostly white from the muck and plaster all over him.

I'm sure I looked the same. No doubt, our time was up.

The Taliban had blown the gate and followed the blast with shooters, who rushed in to kill as many people as possible before meeting their own demise. We had thankfully survived Phase One, but the gunners were preparing for Phase Two.

Huddled behind the counter, I looked at Jackson and he stared back at me. We could not find our words. I took an immediate inventory of my faculties. Eyes, two good ones, check. Nose, intact. I didn't feel blood or wetness anywhere. I counted ten fingers. I was able to see my shoes and move my legs. All limbs and extremities were accounted for.

Our situation was both ironic and embarrassing. Air Traffic Controllers are never lost. We are always composed, known to shake trauma off and regroup. But now, we were shaking like lambs in the woods. We had no clue what was still to come or where it might come from. When the Taliban crashes a party, there are never any negotiations. You are going to meet your maker.

My thoughts were racing: *How did I get here? Will I survive this? Will I see my kids again? Is help on the way? How many Taliban are here? Do I play dead, or do I go for broke and fight? Am I ready to meet God?*

My emotions were clanging and crashing so hard, my mind flipped through all fifty-six years of my life. I had an out of body rush that sent me back to my early days in Mississippi. Growing up, whenever there was violence and mayhem, there was Mom.

Hello, World

Jerry was the first born. I was the second oldest but three years younger. Carl was next and three years younger than me. Lastly, Tommy was the baby, exactly nine years my junior.

My very first memory of life was when Jerry and I were being chased around our shack by one of the neighbors. I must have been close to three years of age, so Jerry was almost six. Mrs. Brunson's husband was trying to keep Jerry and me from intervening in a roaring fight between his wife and my mom. The two ladies weren't pulling any punches. They cursed, screamed, and gouged one another like two shrieking alley cats. I'd like to say that the gloves came off, but it was their clothes instead. They were down to next to nothing, yet the fight continued.

Their clothes weren't the only casualties. The furniture got it too. A chair that used to sit in the corner found its way to the front of the room. Tables were flipped upside down. One minute, Mom seemed to have the upper hand and the next, Mrs. Brunson was in control. Sheer terror engulfed the room.

Mr. Brunson tried to restrain us, but keeping us out of the fight was like trying to corral wild pigs. Jerry would make a grab for Mrs. Brunson's leg and I chomped on her arm with my teeth. Eventually, the police arrived and broke up the fight. Jerry and I walked out with a few minor scrapes, but the mental scars would take years to heal.

The fight at the house that day wasn't the last of the heart-stomping encounters with the Brunsons. Another one took place shortly after the couple moved away. Mom found out where they had gone, and she was determined to get her revenge. She filled some Coke bottles with kerosene, with the plan to burn their house down. Mom took Jerry with her on her mission and left me at home alone in the middle of the night. I was panicking because I was afraid of losing both of them. I was also terrified at the thought that my mom might harm someone, get injured, or even arrested.

After they returned, I quietly asked Jerry what happened. He said Mom had thrown the bottles on the Brunsons' roof, but nothing happened. They didn't explode or burst into flames as she had intended. I was relieved, but felt like a traitor for being happy that Mom had failed to destroy the Brunson home. I never knew if or when she would try something like that again.

Mom's hatred for the Brunsons lasted practically two decades. I'm not sure why they were enemies, but I suspect my mom had slept with Mr. Brunson. As disturbed as she was – and I mean a real whack job – I was shocked that she never got hurt. She never succeeded at inflicting injuries on anyone, either; at least, no one outside our immediate family.

20

They Called Her Liza

My mom's name was Eliza. Everyone called her Liza or Ms. Liza. There were different reactions whenever her name was called: snickers or sometimes laughter, but mostly looks of alarm and concern. The reactions depended on *why* her name was being called and what proximity you were to her.

Ms. Liza was all of 5 feet 2 inches tall, as potent and powerful as a nuclear bomb. People who didn't fear her had no idea how close they were to being maimed, or worse. It was those individuals I prayed for.

Mom was so notorious that whenever bullies were meddling, they called my brothers and me 'Little Liza'. When no one else was around, we teased each other with the same 'Little Liza' chant. It was like when African Americans call each other the N word. You had to be in the family to use the slur. Otherwise you were instigating a fight.

Rumor had it that my mom was given a spiked drink (a mickey) when she was in her early twenties. From then on, she was never right in the head again. She started doing weird things like talking to herself or lashing out at people without cause. I heard the story about the spiked drink several times from unrelated sources, but I never knew what was really wrong with her.

Mom yelled and barked and banged around at home for hours on end until, eventually, she tired herself out. No doubt, I was damaged by her behavior. Prison would have been a peaceful retreat from the antics that unfolded before me on a daily basis. There was no place to run or hide from the things I saw and heard when Ms. Liza was on a tear. She was constantly arguing with the voices in her head.

Against my better judgment, sometimes I got into verbal spats with Mom when she wouldn't pipe down. Her rambling, cursing, and banging always got more intense when she had an audience. Just when I thought I knew what to expect from her, she ad-libbed a new and more chilling twist to her show.

More than once, I foolishly tried to hide or remove shoes, hammers, pots, pans, and a table saw that mom use to accentuate her rants and raves. But as soon as my back was turned, she would bludgeon me with whatever she could get her hands on. Afterwards, I had no choice except to grab my books and haul ass out of there.

When it got really bad, I always ran to Aunt Kathy's house. Aunt Kathy was my mom's sister. She'd bandage me up and let me stay the night, but she always made me go home the next day. Little did I know, Aunt Kathy was the warden of that asylum.

Neither Mom nor Aunt Kathy cared if my grades suffered as a result of my mom's behavior. I wasn't the Golden Child, and I certainly knew it. Jerry was the family's crowned jewel. All my childhood, I wished and wished for a set of encyclopedias. Man, I could have gotten lost for days between the pages. If Jerry had wanted those books, he undoubtedly would have gotten them, but he didn't have the slightest interest in reading or learning.

Of course, Aunt Kathy knew her sister was a lunatic, but everything was all about her and her superficial image. She would say to us that "Mom was crazy," but wouldn't admit as much to anyone else. Her angle was to deny, deny, deny. As much as she tried to hide Mom's problems from other relatives and the community, Aunt Kathy cherished her sister's derangement because it forced us to look up to her, especially her precious little Jerry.

Sadly, Mom worshipped Aunt Kathy more than she worshipped God. She allowed her big sister to control us. I never heard Mom call Aunt Kathy by her real name. It was always, "Sister said to do this," or, "Sister said to do that."

As far as I was concerned, all of my relatives were Dodo birds. There was no avoiding the foolishness that surrounded me. I thought about running away many times, but where would I go? How would I survive? I was only a child. Leaving wasn't a realistic option. I had to endure my situation until I went off to college. Until then, there was no way out.

PART II:
DYSFUNCTION JUNCTION

Chaos Reigns

Dylan was listening intently as I shared the messed up stories from my childhood. Ripping off the bandages from my youth was having a calming effect on me. Either that, or it was the booze. Maybe both. Strangely enough, it felt okay to tell this total stranger the troubling details of my past.

He wanted to hear more about the bombing, which had grabbed his attention. He looked at me in wonder and said, "You're still walking among us. What happened after the initial blast? Did the shooters come rushing in? I would have crapped in my pants and sobbed like a baby."

I laughed a little. "Of course I wanted to cry. The explosion happened so fast; I was scared shitless."

I felt a chill of remembrance and suddenly, I was back behind that counter in the dining hall with Jackson, facing my worst nightmare.

I heard Mike and Ace calling our names. Somehow, we found each other in all the rubble and dust. Everyone was okay except for bumps and bruises. The bad news was, no one had a clue or plan of what to do next.

The silence in the room had all of us on edge. We listened for help; we listened for horrors. I could only make out the popping of broken glass that sounded like gunshots. The waiting made us delirious. We were sitting ducks. We needed to do something besides hide until execution. The question was, what and when? And who would initiate a move?

Out of the darkness, eight Afghanis burst from the kitchen. They had pots and pans covering their heads as they made a beeline through the aisles that separated the tables. They ran out the back door, screaming, "La La La La La La La La La!" I had no idea what the chanting noise meant, but I'd heard similar sounds coming from my mom.

They were not Taliban shooters. They were the kitchen staff, but they scared the crap out of us. They could have easily been working with the Taliban. In Afghanistan, it's impossible to know where people's loyalties lie or if they're just looking out for themselves. Everyone was operating on their own agenda.

As Mike, Ace, Jackson, and I stayed crouched behind the counter, waiting for whatever was coming next, I was reminded again of Mississippi and especially Aunt Kathy. She was someone who had only one set of rules—her own. She was always angling for power, no matter how fleeting or shallow it was. No one ever knew what she'd try to pull, but it was always something."

Burn, Baby Burn

I grew up with burn scars covering thirty percent of my body. Luckily, I was spared the good parts. The story I was told was that Mom left a hot plate filled with boiling water unattended on the floor. I was just a baby, crawling around and crashed into the hot liquid, which spilled onto my fragile body. I held that incident and Mom's recklessness against her for many years.

Aunt Kathy rushed me to the hospital, where I stayed in the burn unit until I was well enough to return home. She also took full advantage of the situation. Mom and I were forever indebted to Aunt Kathy for her heroic behavior. She never passed up a chance to say, "Y'all really owe me a lot," or, "Y'all got to pay me back."

For years, I had a severe nose-bleeding problem. Many a time I needed professional attention, but I hated using Aunt Kathy for transportation. I knew each ride would add to my overdrawn account. She felt we were obligated to her for the rest of our lives. It was a chain that crippled me like being in shackles. We were compelled to work for her like servants at the drop of a hat.

Naturally, I had a complex about my burned skin patches until my late twenties. When I was finally old enough, I viewed them as a badge of honor. I've even been given compliments about my scars.

No Opening Acts Wanted

My brother, Jerry, was handsome, energetic, and quite the attention-getter. He was everything I wasn't. I was a dark-skinned kid and there was nothing special about my appearance to draw you in.

What I lacked in looks, I made up for in brains. I was inquisitive, a sponge for information. My drive annoyed everyone whenever Jerry was around. He was the kid they all wanted to get next to, even though he was as dumb as a lump of wood. I taught myself to read before the age of three. Jerry struggled to read well into the second and third grades.

Jerry had no interests beyond being praised and pampered. Aunt Kathy invited her friends and relatives over to see her adorable, talented nephew. He would dance, smile, sing, and everyone loved it. I would dance, smile, sing, and Aunt Kathy would ask me to move the hell out of the way. I thought we were little dancing bears, but in reality, I was a poor substitute for the main event.

Aunt Kathy hated anyone who dared to befriend us. It was tough to have connections with anyone outside of her, Mom, and my brothers. Aunt Kathy's advice always left me empty and bewildered. She said things like, "You don't need to join the Boy

Scouts. They don't know what they're doing." Or, "The school play is just a bunch of foolishness." I wanted to pursue those activities, but Jerry only wanted to be noticed and admired.

Jerry created a big quandary for Aunt Kathy. She wasn't able to have any kids, so she wanted to adopt Jerry from my mom. She saw him as a form of repayment for all the things she had done for her little sister. Mom refused that settlement. Because of Mom's denial, Aunt Kathy never got beyond her anger and rage. She didn't accept not being allowed to have her cherished little nephew as her own. She spent the rest of her days belittling my mom at every turn, taking every opening to show that she would have been the better parent to Jerry."

The 38-Special & Kid Klepto

Aunt Kathy was the matriarch of the family. Even though she didn't have any children of her own, she claimed to have raised her own brothers and sisters. She was the oldest, and her siblings did bow down to her. She wouldn't have it any other way. Even I looked up to her more than I did my own mom.

Mom was crazy, but she had a shapely figure. Despite her antics, she had no shortage of men. Funny how that worked. Many times, Mom's boyfriends stayed overnight. If a man was around when Aunt Kathy came by, she would berate him and throw him out. I even saw her toss guys out at gunpoint. She'd threaten them and say, "I will shoot you until I can't see you!" I remember thinking, *How is that possible? That's a lot of damn shooting!* But Mom never stood up to Aunt Kathy. She just invited the guy back over the following night.

I loved playing tricks on Mom's men. If I was awake, I was keeping them busy. When they fell asleep, I'd either rob them or steal their car keys. They were constantly looking for their wallets or their keys. Trust me, if I could, I took both. Even though I gave them grief and stole their stuff, I was obviously seeking fatherly attention.

After one too many scavenger hunts for his personal items, one of Mom's friends decided it was time to teach me a lesson. He gave me a few shots of wine. At five years old, I just thought it was good-tasting grape juice, and it didn't take much to send me into a tailspin. I must have gulped down a couple cups of the stuff, and spent the rest of that evening stumbling around, throwing up everything I had eaten for the past month. I didn't test that guy at all after that.

Between my behavior, Aunt Kathy's threats with a deadly weapon, or Mom's lack of balance, the smart guys didn't hang around long. Then came the drunks. They had a bigger passion for alcohol than anything or anyone else. They all smoked, and none of them had a car.

There was one guy named Bo. It took years for me to like him. The fact that he was a Joe Frazier fan and I was a Muhammad Ali fan didn't help his cause. Whenever I saw Bo, he was always drunk. I'm sure he even drank on the job. I never saw him without a bottle or a cigarette in his hand. But the more he hung around, the more we engaged. He was actually a fairly smart guy. I learned a lot from him. Looking back, he stimulated my mind more than any man I had ever been around.

Finally, there was Ezell, who worked the grounds at the Friendship Cemetery across the street. I hated him from the start. He smelled. He was almost always drunk. He smoked, and he lied. There was nothing to like about him. The only time I felt sorry for Ezell was when Aunt Kathy came over to threaten him. He must have had nerves of steel to withstand her gun waving, or maybe he was too drunk to care. He saw Aunt Kathy's 38 Special so often, I'm sure he could point it out in a lineup. Maybe that was what Mom liked about him; he stood his ground. I hardly said a word to the guy.

When I was in my twenties, I began to realize what a piss-ant I'd been about Mom's social life. I decided to accept Ezell, who had stuck around all those years, even with his shortcomings. I was long gone from living in the house by then, so it was easier to tolerate him. We became mildly friendly and talked on occasion.

One time, Ezell called to ask if I had any clothes he could borrow. He wanted to take my mom to church and look presentable. All he had was grubby work clothes from the cemetery. I had plenty of quality suits I didn't wear anymore. So, I had them tailored and shipped to Ezell. He loved me for his new look, and after that we got along pretty well whenever I was home.

When Ezell passed away in 2014, I shed a tear. He'd been with Mom for nearly thirty years. When he passed, Mom was not the only one who lost a friend. I did, too.

Two Wheels Only

Around 1965, Mom made the mistake of telling Aunt Kathy she wanted to buy a car. Secretly, I was afraid of being in a car with Mom, but I was still a kid, and cars were exciting. Plus, I was tired of trying to keep up with her on her speed walks to work. Mom worked as a maid at several homes across Columbus. Our primary mode of transportation was walking from one house to another.

We took my baby brother, Carl, to the sitter, and met the car owner at Aunt Kathy's house. It was a late 50s Chevrolet – a little old, but in good condition – and a better car than what Aunt Kathy drove. The three of us went out for a test drive. From a kid's viewpoint, Mom did remarkably well. She had a proud look about her; a look I never saw again after that day. She just knew that car was going to be her new transportation, and I'd already laid claim to the shotgun seat.

When the drive was over, Aunt Kathy abruptly shattered Mom's hopes. She said, "No, no, no. This isn't the car for you." Aunt Kathy made all the major decisions in our household. It was crushing. Mom just allowed Aunt Kathy to kill her dream.

Not only did she kill the dream and the deal, but Aunt Kathy took a large portion of the money Mom had saved to buy the car. Aunt Kathy always had to get her cut. She controlled absolutely everything and knew what was in Mom's bank account at all times. Later, when I was grown up and working, Aunt Kathy constantly probed me to find out if and when I sent money home. If she had a hunch that Mom had a tiny bit extra, Aunt Kathy showed up to demand her share.

Mom said nothing the entire walk home. I was the noisy one. I kept asking, "Mom, are you going to get that car? Are you thinking about something else?" She never said a word to me.

After Mom's failed attempt to get a car, she went out and bought a bicycle. Lord only knows how she got that one past Aunt Kathy, but ultimately, Mom became known all over town as 'That Crazy Bicycle Lady'.

Ghosts and Dead Dogs

I tend to think that God created dreams mainly for children. Only adults try to interpret their meaning. Kids like myself lived for the nighttime and the dreams that came with it. I could go wherever I wanted, whenever I wanted. I could be the person no one allowed me to be when I was awake. All I needed to do was fall asleep.

Some nights, I left the universe. One time, I was having tea with the sultry Uhura from Star Trek. She took time away from her intergalactic missions just to be my date. She had my undivided attention, and she thought I was funny.

Uhura kept pouring it on. She even promised to visit me when I started elementary school at Mitchell Memorial. I wanted to show her off to the other kids at school. I was so taken with her, I was going bonkers. I stuck out my chest like a proud rooster and started talking trash just to impress her. I assured Uhura she had nothing to worry about. "Leave those space creatures to me. Trust me, I'll fight them off for you."

Uhura reached out and shook me. She called me Howard. I was confused because that is not my name, but she kept shaking me and saying, "Howard, Howard, wake up." Why would Uhura be shaking me so roughly?

Suddenly, I opened my eyes. Mom was trying to get me out of bed. Of course, it had to be Mom. She was the only one who called me Howard. (I hated that name. Aunt Kathy gave me my real name, but Mom couldn't pronounce it.)

Mom wanted to know if I had heard any noises. I was still trying to shake myself awake.

"What noises?" I asked. She said, "Listen, just listen!"

I tried to sharpen my senses so I could tune into what Mom was hearing. I tilted my head to my strongest ear and became motionless while zeroing in on all sounds. I got nothing.

Mom said, "Those ghosts and dead dogs are walking through the house." I was startled by her statement and on edge, but I didn't hear or see anything that indicated there were ghosts or dead dogs in the house. Mom followed me with her eyes as I went from room to room, trying to locate the intruders. Finally, I gave up and said, "There's nothing here."

It was like I had given her the green light for a full-scale showcase. Mom dove into an array of curses and shouts like nothing I had ever heard before. I was too shocked to move. She was so convincing, I wanted to help her fend off the spirits she was yelling at, but what could I do? I teared up out of fear and felt hopeless. I was only six years old—no match for the spirits in Mom's head.

After she ranted and raved for more than an hour, up one wall and down another, she finally came to a stop. She'd unleashed pure verbal mayhem and exhausted herself. Usually, that was the only way her battle against the ghosts and dead dogs came to an end.

My Thank-less Thanksgiving Dinner

I was short and very skinny for most of my childhood. My teeth were brown, with little indentations. No doubt, I was malnourished. We never had any food at our house, let alone healthy food. But Aunt Kathy had plenty. I'm not sure where she got it all, but she had two loaded refrigerators and two loaded freezers. There were cakes, candy, cookies, and fruits to a kid's delight. For all her abundance, she wouldn't allow me or my little brother Carl to eat any of it. Only Jerry received those treats. The fruit never got eaten. It rotted in the bowl.

Needless to say, I never wanted to be around there for any amount of time. Aside from all the food, her house was also stuffed with fine furniture and exotic trinkets. Aunt Kathy's house was a nice place, but it was also a reminder of what I couldn't touch or have. Plus, the place smelled from rotting food and outdated produce. I hated being there.

I resented Aunt Kathy's cooking as much as her withholding food from us. Her cooking was almost as rotten as the fruit and vegetables in her kitchen. We were hungry, but we didn't want any part of her meals. Nevertheless, Aunt Kathy insisted on hosting Thanksgiving. She invited her friends, co-workers, and church members over to show off her house and her cute little nephew, Jerry. It was more like a summons that couldn't be refused.

When Mom, Carl, and me got to Aunt Kathy's, Jerry greeted us at the door with glee. He acted like the little lord of the manor and wanted to show us around. Maybe he'd forgotten that I'd already been there a million times before, working in the yard and cleaning the inside of the house every weekend since I could walk. I knew Aunt Kathy's house like the back of my hand.

Jerry was dressed liked a stage performer. Since my own attire was a thread above hobo level, I couldn't help but wonder where my matching outfit was. No one told us, but this Thanksgiving was "The Jerry Show." Of course, my act didn't make the program.

Everyone kissed up to Aunt Kathy and exclaimed, "How wonderful that little Jerry boy is!" I got a quarter to stay out of the way. I mentally calculated how many quarters I could collect just by keeping my mouth shut if we took "The Jerry Show" on the road.

When it was time for dinner, the non-family guests left. Aunt Kathy took her seat at the head of the table with Jerry on her right. Carl sat between Mom and me, on her left. Mom's cooking (if you could call it that) was terrible, but Aunt Kathy's cooking was truly wretched.

Thanksgiving is no time for amateur hour in the kitchen, but we were subjected to this Gong Show on a yearly basis. Aunt Kathy went knee deep in her preparations where others would have surrendered.

She even tried to make biscuits, pies, and cakes from scratch.

She always served baked turkey, glazed ham, turnip greens, potato salad, rice pudding, black tea, and chitterlings. Carl and I sat at attention while Jerry practically narrated the meal. We were hostages to "The Jerry and Aunt Kathy Brouhaha." Jerry said, "Aunt Kathy cooked the turkey," while she smiled at him with approval. I knew from past experience, the turkey was always dry enough to gag a gorilla, so I wasn't going there.

When he said, "Aunt Kathy made the greens," she chimed in, "Those turnips are mustard greens with fat-back. Harold, you need to eat these. You may be puny but that fat-back will help you grow. Eat up, now." I had no choice but to gulp down this cloudy, meatless glob of animal fat. It was like trying to swallow a gelatin block of mineral oil or a giant booger.

After I regained consciousness, I was told to try the chitterlings. I strongly declined. They were in the "No Way, No How" category. (For those who weren't raised in the South, chitterlings are made from the intestines of a pig or other animal.) They would have had to beat me repeatedly before I tried those chitterlings. No Way, No How was I going to sample anything that looked and smelled liked a bowel movement.

Mom offered the rice pudding, which she had made, so it was in the treacherous category. I hated the stuff anyway and passed again. Finally, I asked for the ham and the potato salad, and told them to pass those items to Carl as well. They were the only edible food on the whole Thanksgiving table.

When I looked up, Jerry was chomping down on Aunt Kathy's dry turkey breast. He looked liked a billy goat trying to swallow the tongue of a leather boot. That piece of meat just wouldn't go down. Like I said, I wasn't going there.

My main concern was collecting some of the packaged cakes, cookies, and candies Aunt Kathy had lying around. I wore loose fitting clothes, specifically to grab and stash some items 'to go' for me and Carl. I knew I could count on Mom to provide the necessary distraction. As predicted, she got up from the table and headed out back to look at the garden. Since I worked in that garden almost every weekend, I knew there wasn't much to see. It had recently been plowed for the season but at its best, it produced corn, potatoes, turnip greens, string beans, tomatoes, and peanuts.

Aunt Kathy never trusted Mom unattended. When she got up to keep an eye on Mom, Jerry, of course, followed along. They were gone just long enough for me to have my way with the cakes, cookies, and candies all over the dining room. I made sure to also grab what Carl wanted, to keep him silent.

Once back inside, Mom walked the house from room to room. Our visits always ended the same way, with Mom looking around for something to swipe. Aunt Kathy knew it, too. They argued until Aunt Kathy threw Mom out. I didn't like the fights, but it meant we could finally get out of there.

Aunt Kathy sent us home with leftovers unfit for a dog. I played along, and always asked for extra take-aways just to make her feel good. Then I dumped the stuff before we got home. Just like all occasions at Aunt Kathy's, Carl and me were in for a long night of battling over the john. I spent many holidays caressing the toilet to relieve myself of Aunt Kathy's efforts.

PART III:
SCRAPPER

Every Man for Himself

Dylan was traveling back in history with me, but my near-death encounter in Afghanistan was heavy on his mind. He laughed in solidarity over the Aunt Kathy stories, then moved the conversation back to the Afghanis tearing out of the kitchen with pots and pans on their heads. Knowing the story didn't end there, he wanted to know what happened next.

I confirmed that we were white-knuckle scared of impending death. Even though those guys who ran out the kitchen were the food servers, we had no way of knowing whose side they were on. We were on high alert for a "Green on Blue" attack, which is when an insider opens fire on coalition forces. Running out of the kitchen and into the aisles could have been a setup to get us to come out of hiding.

Despite the risks, Mike, Ace, and Jackson decided to go for it and make a dash for 'the safe room' inside the barracks. They followed the Afghani servers out the door, covering their heads with their arms. I gave the room one final look over and raced behind my coworkers to the exit. I didn't want to stick around by myself to find out what was coming next.

I was the oldest of the air traffic controllers, but no slouch athletically. Nevertheless, they left me at the starting blocks as if I was asleep when the referee said, "Go." When I made it to the exit door, no one was in sight. They had gotten the hell out of there faster than my head could spin.

I saw nothing and no one outside the door. The popping sound of glass became much louder, but I was determined to survive this ordeal.

I reminded myself, I was a born scrapper. If I could survive my childhood and my family, I could survive a surprise Taliban bombing. Even my early social interactions had been a battle back in Mississippi.

The 6-Year-Old Flirt

At six years old, I couldn't wait to start school. For three years, I had watched Jerry leave home every day with a smile, minus any books or academic utensils. He came home with an even bigger smile, along with borrowed paper, borrowed pencils, and other kids' work assignments. The kids yelled his name in the streets, and Jerry started making friends beyond his brothers. (Of course, Aunt Kathy had sinful labels for each and every child that tried to befriend her precious Jerry.)

I got the impression that school was a joyous place, and interrogated Jerry every day. I wanted to know all I could about school. I wanted to know about the teachers, the students, his friends, and finally, the girls. Even at nine years old, Jerry knew all the pretty girls.

Jerry didn't offer many details about the teachers, he knew even less about being a student, and he was very protective of his friends. In other words, he wasn't willing to share any of it with me. Yet, he didn't mind talking about the girls. I was spellbound. I wanted to meet pretty girls just like my big brother. I wanted to know what to do and what to say. I kept pestering him for details. I told him he had to give me some pointers so I wouldn't look bad.

Suddenly, he snapped, "You can't be like me. I'm Jerry!" I didn't know what that meant, but would soon find out.

After days of being a nuisance, Jerry gave in and shared a small tip about how to handle the girls. He said, "As you walk past the girls, just tip your hat and smile." Like a star pupil, I committed that nugget to my social repertoire.

On my first day of school, I left home with glee and determination. I had a pep in my step and a song in my heart. On the way, I came upon a set of female twins named Mary and Martha. They were walking slowly in my direction. They had to be about nine years old, and may as well have been five feet, nine inches tall, whereas I was only six years old and stood four feet even. Their age and height didn't matter, though. I saw them as two full glasses of lemonade.

Since it was the dead of summer, I was wearing a cap to shield my face from the hot Mississippi sun. As I approached the twins I smiled, tipped my hat, and continued on my way. I had done the 'big move' just as Jerry instructed. I smiled from jawline to jawline; I was so full of myself.

Out of nowhere, one of the twins grabbed my cap while the other delivered a blow to my head. She slapped the taste right out of my mouth. I couldn't even feel my tongue. I spun around to face my bullies. The twins had become triplets. I couldn't remember ever trying to drink three glasses of anything and this wouldn't be the day to try. The girls stared at me and said, "Who the hell do you think you are?"

The third girl disappeared. She was a mirage, a figment of my imagination; created when I was knocked senseless. I shrugged and stared back at the twins. They gave me back my cap and told me to get lost. I didn't challenge those instructions.

So much for Jerry's advice! I needed to create my own playbook.

Money or No Money

Almost everyone in the Red Line Community was on some type of welfare. We were poster kids for the program. Most families were too embarrassed to admit they received assistance, even though we all needed it.

Those who thought they were better off shamed anyone they saw using food stamps (SNAPS). In our community, the need for food stamps was just another opportunity to humiliate each other. Since Mom didn't shop or cook, she gave us the coupons so we could feed ourselves.

Imagine what an unsupervised seven-year-old buys for breakfast or dinner. I had chips, candy, cookies, and sodas day after day. I'm sure my junk food addiction stunted my growth and rotted my teeth.

The local stores that accepted SNAPS coupons gave a credit or 'due bill' that looked like a sales receipt. Instead of giving change in dollars or coins, 'due bills' insured your return to the same grocer. A receipt was just a record of what you bought, but a due bill was left over money to spend. In essence, the store was guaranteed to get the rest of your Food Stamp funds.

Jerry and I played a running joke on our younger brother, Carl. We sent him out shopping with sales receipts instead of due bills, knowing he would get rejected. To add an extra punch to the prank, we told Carl to pick out something he really wanted. We knew the outcome long before Carl even left the house. Our biggest challenge was keeping our faces straight, but once he was out the door, we fell into stitches.

Carl would come back from the store empty handed, with tears streaming down his face. Sadly, his reaction was just the motivation we needed to keep pulling the stunt on him. Occasionally, we gave him the real due bill just to make sure the trick had longevity. It was awfully mean to haze our own little brother like that, but he gave me some of the best laughs of my childhood.

Beat His Marbled Ass

One of the cheapest and most fun games we played was shooting marbles. All the stores sold them, either in packs or individually. The Big Mama was an oversized marble; an anomaly. No one really wanted it but we all had one. There were Bumble Bees and Cat Eyes, too. Mostly everyone wanted the Bumble Bees.

Shooting marbles was a sport, but it was also a gambling addiction. Many parents didn't allow their kids to shoot marbles because it could get so cutthroat. I had no supervision and even less entertainment at home, so I practiced shooting marbles from sunrise to sunset. I got to be pretty good and acquired quite a collection by winning marbles off of other kids.

I was only a second grader, yet I got some respect when it came to the game. Our elementary was divided into the lower level (grades one through three) and the upper level (grades four through six). The lower level was barred from playing at the upper level at all times. That restriction was for me as well, but I was beating all the kids in the lower so profoundly, my only competition was with the older boys at the upper level.

One morning before school started, I heard the upper level kids playing marbles. Yes! I thought.

Another chance to take those suckers down. But I'd left my marble bag at home. I only needed a few marbles to get into the game. There was a fish tank in the classroom across from my homeroom—it was lined with marbles. I walked in, rolled up my sleeves, took four marbles out of the tank, went up to the restricted upper level, and beat those guys senseless.

By 8 a.m., I had about forty new marbles for my collection. I was so happy with my take, I was whistling and walking to homeroom with sheer joy in my heart. It was time for class, but no one was there when I walked in. Everyone was gathered in the room across the hall; the room with the fish tank where I had stolen the marbles.

Mrs. Dorothy, the second-grade teacher, was ripping Jerry a new one. The school teachers in 1967 were not shy about outright beating students to keep us in line. These days they'd call it child abuse, but back then it was standard operating procedure. Most of the kids, myself included, were deathly afraid of the teachers. We'd all seen them inflict some real damage.

Mrs. Dorothy was six feet, two inches tall and tipped the scales at about two hundred pounds. No one, and I mean no one, dared to mess with Mrs. Dorothy. Even students in the other grades were not safe from her if they got into trouble. I caught Jerry's eyes and silently mouthed, "Please don't tell! Oh God, please don't tell!" Usually, he would do anything to sell me down the river, but this time he kept his mouth shut.

There was no way I was going to come clean after seeing the shake down Mrs. Dorothy delivered to Jerry. When she was through with him, Mrs. Dorothy moved on to another boy, named Sonny Lincoln. Sonny was known as the most disobedient child in the second grade. Someone had fingered him and Jerry for taking the marbles out of the fish tank.

Before she even got to him, Sonny was crying, pleading, and imploring for someone to believe his innocence. Mrs. Dorothy grabbed him by the arm and Sonny went crashing to the floor. He was screaming, "It wasn't me! It wasn't me, Mrs. Dorothy!" Mrs. Dorothy lost her grip on Sonny's hand and he quickly headed for the door. Mrs. Dorothy rebounded and slammed the door on Sonny's left foot. Sonny was digging and digging for traction with his right leg like a car stuck in the mud. He was shouting, "Oh Lord, Oh Lord!" Mrs. Dorothy found some compassion for a fleeting moment. She let up on Sonny's foot, which allowed him to escape the building, but Mrs. Dorothy got in her car and ran Sonny down. She brought him back before the classroom and finished beating Sonny like a busted snare drum.

For me, this was too much — way, way too much. Hell yes, I quit playing marbles at school after that.

Holidays from Hell

There was never anything great about the holidays growing up, except getting a break from school. Yes, I got the warm fuzzy feeling of the season and enjoyed the shop displays, but that was where it ended. For me, there was nothing else to look forward to. Mom didn't delve into holiday preparations on any level. Her go-to was the Salvation Army or whatever extras her employers gave her. Being that mom worked as a maid, the homeowners gave her food and donations when they had too much. Yes, I ate whatever food she was lucky enough to receive, but the thought that other people or organizations dictated my holiday happiness bothered me. I resented my mom's frame of mind and the fact that she couldn't get it together, even for Christmas.

Every year, there was a campaign on the local TV station for kids to write to Santa Claus. I jumped on it like a kid possessed. I even bought my own stamps and envelopes. I always got my letter in earlier than the year before. In fact, I sent multiple letters, in case Santa's elves misplaced the original.

On Christmas Eve, I followed all of the rituals of putting milk and cookies out for Santa and getting to bed early. On Christmas Day, I was stunned and brokenhearted that Santa had missed our house. I didn't know if I was a bad child, or if he was afraid of Mom, or if he ran short of gifts. Like all kids at Christmas, I was definitely in denial about being on the bad list.

I specifically remember asking Mom one Christmas, "Where are our gifts? What about Carl and Tommy?" (Tommy was my youngest brother; six years younger than Carl, nine years younger than me.) "Carl's been good and Tommy's just a baby. Why didn't Santa come to our house for them?"

She said, "You can each have an orange." Even the fruit came from the Salvation Army or a church donation. The whole thing was a joke between Carl and me.

My lead-in was, "Hey, Carl, I have your Christmas gift. It's really special. You're going to love it," while I hid a piece of fruit behind my back.

He never took the bait on this one. He said, "Yeah, right."

Then, I offered him a gift-wrapped orange or apple or whatever else was lying around. Of course, he would try to pull the same trick on me at a later time.

I always told myself that next year would be the 'big one'. Santa would come and make up for years past. In the meantime, I saw a parade of kids with new toys and new bicycles, wearing big smiles that would melt even the toughest Grinch's heart. I couldn't wait for the holidays to be over.

Tales of a Fourth-Grade Nothing

Until I had schoolwork of my own, I did Jerry's homework for him on a daily basis. He was three grades ahead of me, but school was never his thing. He really started to tank in the fourth grade. He was never around to actually go to school, because he went everywhere with Aunt Kathy. She made all the rounds that were noteworthy to her, taking Jerry to the supermarket, the county fair, the mall, and church conferences. They went all over Columbus together.

All the moments Jerry spent with Aunt Kathy short-circuited any hope of Jerry ever opening a book or completing his homework. Jerry saw these outing as his Play Time while Aunt Kathy use them as her personal Expo. Everyone all over Columbus got to know Jerry. Aunt Kathy made sure of that. Aunt Kathy used Jerry's good looks as a way to win over her peers, church members, and co-workers.

Subsequently, Jerry failed the fourth grade. Some kids struggle in school, but failing a grade was not common. For Jerry, school was just a roll of the dice. When word got out, Carl and I were stunned by the news. At the time I didn't think failing a grade in elementary was even possible.

People started talking around town, so Aunt Kathy

came over and poured out on Mom. She blamed Mom for Jerry's collapse, for not teaching him better, and for not helping with his homework. She blamed Mom for not being good at anything.

If anyone was to blame, it was Aunt Kathy herself. She was too busy parading Jerry around like a show pony. He was living with Aunt Kathy almost entirely, so he wasn't around for me to help even if he decided to crack open a book.

Carl was about three years old at the time, so he started to cry from all of Aunt Kathy's yelling and cussing. I had to remove him from the scene because Aunt Kathy wouldn't let up.

After Aunt Kathy's tongue lashing, Mom got Jerry, Carl, and me together for a school visit. The four of us headed to Mitchell Memorial Elementary to see Jerry's teacher, Mrs. Lewis. I knew a storm was brewing.

It was late on a Friday afternoon, and luckily, classes were over for the day. Mom walked into Mrs. Lewis' classroom unannounced. The teacher took one look at our motley crew and asked, "How can I help you, Ma'am?"

Mom went straight for it. She said, "Ha, I'll tell you how the hell you can help me! You can let those dogs and devils go and put Jerry in the right grade."

Calmly, Mrs. Lewis said, "Oh, you must be Jerry's mother."

Mom fired back, "Yeah, I'm his momma! Why in the hell are you holding him back?"

Mrs. Lewis responded, "No Ma'am, I'm not holding

him back. Jerry failed because he didn't do the work that's required of a fourth grader. If he can't do the work here, then sending him to the next level is a disservice to him, the students, and the teachers of the fifth grade."

Mom unleashed the beast. "I don't care about your service. Put my boy where he belongs so those dogs, devils, ghosts, and haints will leave him alone. Those dogs are knocking at you! Just listen! Listen!"

Mrs. Lewis had the most bewildered look on her face. I looked at Carl, and he smirked back at me. We knew Mom was taking Mrs. Lewis someplace she didn't know how to handle. Mom went to the chalkboard and started to bang on it profusely while saying, "Those dogs are barking at you, baby. They got you and my boy."

Fortunately, the principal walked by as this scene was unfolding. He stepped into the room and asked, "What is going on in here?"

I reached out to shield Carl from that crazy man. He had put the fear of God in me so often that I instinctively feared for my little brother as well.

Mom explained, "Dogs, devils, and haints got this teacher. She is holding my Jerry back!"

It was the principal's turn to give Mom a bewildered look. He put down his can of soda and asked for a minute while he talked to Mrs. Lewis. The teacher pulled out a pile of papers. They were Jerry's tests and homework assignments. Mrs. Lewis said, "Ma'am, here is the proof that Jerry isn't up to a fourth grade level. He has an F on several of these assignments. In fact, a zero grade is too high for some of Jerry's work this last year."

That's when Mom went nuclear. She said, "I got your zero and your ass right here," as she balled up her fists.

The principal tried to temper things down. He said, "Ma'am, Ma'am, we're sorry, but this is where Jerry is right now. As a matter of fact, we're not sure how Jerry even got this far."

I had never thought of Mom as being funny before, but she responded with, "Jerry got here by getting up, getting on the bus, and walking into this damn class!"

The principal and Mrs. Lewis just stared at each other in silence. Then, Mom picked up the principal's soda can and gulped down what was left of it. To me, that was a big warning. Quickly, I moved Carl to a safer area. I was envisioning wildfires, tornados, flash floods, and a tsunami coming next, but Mom surprised us all. She calmly asked, "Why can't Jerry go to summer school to make up for his lack of achievements?"

The principal and Mrs. Lewis said in unison Jerry was too far behind for summer classes. He would have to repeat the year, and Mrs. Lewis didn't look too happy about that.

Once again, to my disbelief, Mom stood up and bolted out of the room. Jerry followed her with the same haste. He never said one word the entire time. Carl and I were left alone. I grabbed my little brother and backpedaled out of the room. I didn't want to stick around to find out if the principal had any residual punishments for us.

Jerry's fate was sealed. School became just a place he went to socialize and stir up trouble. He would eventually fizzle out in middle school. But for that moment in time, he was a true tale of a fourth grade nothing.

Get Him, Mom!

Jerry's extra time with Aunt Kathy helped Carl and me grow closer. We created our own games and developed our own jokes. Carl enjoyed reading along as I did my schoolwork. We started to do more things together and spent a lot of time away from the house. Mainly, we were bored and looking for something to do. Sometimes we were in search of something to eat like plums, pears, peaches, or watermelon. Those fruits grow plentifully in Mississippi; you just have to know where to find them.

We were on our way home from one of our outings when Carl's classmate persuaded us to climb up into a neighbor's pear tree. It didn't take a lot of convincing, because the classmate was awfully cute and we were already looking for fruit. Within minutes, the homeowner showed up and caught us up in his pear tree. He was furious.

The man forced Carl and me into his truck. He drove us around to his friends and his family who took turns cussing and threatening to beat us. I kept my poker face the whole time, which angered them even more. It was obvious they were trying to scare us to tears. It worked on Carl, but not on me. They kept levying all sorts of attacks at me, hoping I would fold under their insults.

Finally, the man drove us home. He said he was going to get our mom to whip us for our behavior. I was grinning slightly because little did he know, our nightmare would soon become his. I was all in for some horrors to fall upon this guy. I didn't appreciate him making my little brother cry either.

When we got to our house, Carl and I jumped out of the truck and ran inside. We didn't have to say a word. Before the man could even present Mom with our transgressions, she was cussing, attacking, and throwing things at him and his truck. She was yelling about the dead dogs and devils. It was the only time I was delighted to see Mom go from zero to crazy! The man got the hell out of there as fast as he could.

No Starter Pistol

When I was nine years old and Carl was six, Mom bought a .22 pistol. Whenever there is a gun in the house, kids will find it like a tornado finds a trailer park. Carl and I played with Mom's pistol whenever she left for work. We took the bullets out and practiced aiming it.

Surprisingly, we never fired it or got hurt. Carl and I fought a lot because he had a smart mouth. If I punched him out, he would get Mom's gun and chase after me.

I had my own psychotic moment with Mom's gun. I was out practicing marbles when a group of teenagers stopped by to belittle me. They were hurling insults about Ms. Liza, "That Crazy Bicycle Lady."

Not one to accept ridicule, I ran inside to get mom's gun. Instead of them scattering and running away like I hoped, they huddled behind each other. Just as I took aim to scare them, I was attacked from behind. It took about twenty minutes before one of the guys was able to disarm me.

Shortly after the incident, Aunt Kathy came and took Mom's gun away. It was the smartest thing Aunt Kathy ever did.

A Bullet Has No Name

Mom's pistol was soon replaced with a .22 rifle she kept in the closet. I'm not sure why she felt she needed a gun in the house, but it didn't take long for her to find an occasion to use it.

The following summer, our house was under siege by a pack of bullying teenagers. We were easy targets because of Ms. Liza and her crazy behavior. The teenagers who came after us were bold, bored, and just plain stupid. They were also relentless.

Jerry, Carl, and me were playing outside one day when the teenagers came by to taunt us. Instead of engaging, we went inside for the evening. Like moths to a flame, the teens followed us. They started throwing rocks against the house. They wanted to draw Mom out for one of her many shows. She peeped her head out of the door a few times to tease them, but she wasn't giving them the full spectacle they had come for.

They were desperate for her appearance, so they started dashing to the front door and banging on it. It was as if they had paid money for a performance. They wouldn't quit. They started chanting, "Liza! Liza! Liza!" Normally, Mom would have risen for a curtain call, but that night she stayed quiet with a troubling grin.

After more than any of us could take, she reached for her rifle. The next time the teens banged on the door, Mom fired a shot at the door, but the bullet ricocheted and bounced back to hit Jerry in the shoulder. It was like a scene from a firefight. Jerry screamed, I screamed, and Carl screamed too.

Jerry was rushed to the hospital, where it was discovered the bullet had only broken his skin. He would be okay, but the cops came to the house and took Mom's rifle away. It was her last hurrah as a gun owner. God was definitely looking out for all the fools involved.

Shooting Hooky

I always liked school; probably because I could control how much attention I got. Plus, there was nothing for me to do at home. I had no real friends, no toys, and no cable TV. There wasn't any food, either, so I looked forward to the free lunches. Years later, I never missed a day of high school, but in the second grade, Jerry talked me into playing hooky.

On the day in question, we made a hut out of straw and tree branches just inside the Palmer Home Orphanage's gates, across the street. Our plan was to hide there until Mom left for work, which is what we were doing when we got a surprise visit. Some older dropouts spotted us when we went into our hideout. They crashed through our roof and forced us out. A kid called Emp-man led this pack of hoods. I'd seen him around many times. He looked like a leftover Jack-O-Lantern or a throwaway cartoon.

Emp-man ordered his guys to tackle us and the next thing we knew, he was standing over us with his pants down! I nearly crapped my underwear, cried like a baby, and squealed like a pig. The hoods brought us to our feet and sized us up like we were hamburgers and french fries. We had no idea what this display was all about, but it didn't bode well for us.

I'd seen male packages before. The kids at school

had pissing contests all the time when the teachers weren't paying attention. I never won any challenges, but I was okay with my presentation. And I'd seen some of Mom's boyfriends relieve themselves outside. Seeing their junk wasn't what startled me; what worried me was *why*? I knew plenty of demented hoodrats, but I'd never heard of anything like this before.

Jerry and I locked eyes and tried to make a silent escape plan. I thought about punching Emp-man in the crown jewels as hard as I could, and making a run for it. I knew his goons would chase me down and beat me beyond recognition, but I was willing to take the risk. The only thing that saved Emp-man's balls (and my ass) was my concern for Jerry. He wasn't as well versed in getting his butt whooped as I was and he was nowhere near as fast a runner.

We needed a Godsend, a gift from heaven. Like the answer to our prayers, we heard Mom leaving the house across the street. When the door slammed shut, we started screaming, "Mom, Mom, Help! Mom, Mom! Please help!"

Emp-man and his boys vanished faster than they had appeared. No one, not even crazy Emp-man, wanted a run-in with Ms. Liza. I never saw any of those guys ever again. Looking back, I realize Mom was a necessary evil who kept most of the predators away.

That was the first, the last, and the only time I ever played hooky from school.

Stealing Time

After years of seeing other kids with toys I wanted but didn't have, I learned to hustle. When I was eight years old, I started running errands, picking fruit, or doing lawn care. My jobs gave me the cash to buy a G.I. Joe, Hot Tracks, and Rock 'Em Sock 'Em Robots. The toys made me feel normal, but I had to put in a lot of time and hard work to get what I wanted.

One day, I saw a watch in a local department store. I just had to have it, so I made it my target and saved all my money to get that watch. I went into overdrive. I ran errand after errand. I doubled my load of picking fruit. I raked leaves and cut hedges like a kid possessed. Eventually, I was able to buy the $14 Timex. I was so proud of myself.

On the very day I bought the watch, I was stopped near my house by a thug called Goat Turd. This guy was about fifteen years old and a constant terror in the community. Very casually, he asked me what time it was. I peered at my Timex while keeping my distance, and gave him the time. Goat Turd said he had to *see* the time. I held my arm out so he could see my watch, then quickly tried to make my way into the house.

He grabbed me and held me in the air while he tried to strip the Timex off my wrist. I was kicking and screaming and keeping a death grip on my watch. Suddenly, Goat Turd bit my arm so hard I couldn't take the pain. Finally, I relented and yelled, "Take it. Just take it!" He unbuckled my watchband and disappeared out of sight.

I ran inside wailing and shouting, but no one was home to help me. I wanted to call the police in the worst way, but we didn't have a phone. I ran to a neighbor's house and called the Columbus Police Department to report the crime.

When the cops came out, they asked if I could identify my assailant. I knew exactly where Goat Turd lived, so they put me in the cruiser and we drove over. I walked inside, escorted by the officers. Goat Turd was just sitting there wearing my Timex as his own fashion statement.

My description was so spot on, the cops didn't even consider Goat Turd's defense. They got my watch back, handcuffed him, and led him out of the house. I smiled at him and said, "Looks like now you'll be doing time, instead of stealing it." He sneered at me and the cops laughed at my wit.

A Moment in the Sun

Because of Mom's unpredictable behavior, I had no confidence in her ability to be anything more than a sideshow.

In the second grade, the teachers sent a memo home calling for parent participation in the annual talent show. Due to Jerry's sloppiness or my own, Mom discovered the notice. He and I went into overdrive to convince her she didn't need to join in, but Mom would have none of it. She was hell bent on performing even though she had nothing to offer, as far as we knew.

Jerry could dance but none of us could sing, and we definitely did not want Mom trying to sing or dance in front of the whole school. Just the thought of her involvement gave us anxiety attacks. We tried every lie and excuse in the book to keep her away, but we were overruled. For Mom, this was her big moment.

On the night of the dreaded event, I asked Jerry what he was planning to do. Hell, I wasn't even sure what I was going to do. We hadn't rehearsed, there had been no dry run, and we had no idea what Mom had in mind.

When we got to school, Mom kept Jerry close to her. She knew I was a stray cat, so she didn't even bother trying to control me. I wandered around looking for a good place to hide. I was picturing all the embarrassment that would ensue before, during, and after this fiasco.

When the time came, the three of us gathered backstage behind the curtain. Mind you, I was tearing slightly because of the near certain death of my already dismal social life. When the curtains rolled back, Mom and Jerry took center stage. I tried to find a spot where I would be shielded from the audience. There were snickers and a few spots of laughter at the sight of "That Crazy Bicycle Lady." My heart was beating louder than the audience's rumble. The principal signaled for everyone to settle down.

What happened next left me stunned. Mom stood out there on the stage and recited The Gettysburg Address in its entirety. She did it dynamically and flawlessly, without a single stumble. She was rewarded with a raucous standing ovation.

I have never been more proud of her than I was that night. I have no idea how she pulled it off, or where her calm delivery came from. It must have been a trick leftover from her own school days, before someone slipped her a mickey and she went off the rails.

Of course, the glow was only temporary. The next day, Mom was up to her old tricks of humiliating and shaming me all over town. But for that solitary moment, it felt so good to see Mom shine.

Happy Halloween

As a kid, I saw Fright Night as the great equalizer of holiday enjoyment. All I needed was a mask and a container to collect my candy. I knew where to go and what techniques were needed for a trove of goodies. I went to grocery stores, corner markets, schools, churches, and breezed through all the upscale communities. My Trick-or-Treat sack was just a plastic bag from the grocery store, but my Halloween haul was so big, it required additional assistance to carry and at least two or three trips back to the house to unload.

My diet was bad enough as it was, but Halloween was a windfall for me. That one night gave me enough candy to last until Christmas. I'm sure my disciplinary infractions increased from November to January due to the sugar intake. I was hyper all the time.

I used my candy stash as a way to make extra money. I sold it at cut-rate prices and was known as "The Big Negotiator." Candy even kept the bullies at bay.

The only person I couldn't control with my stash was Mom. She had a sugar tooth that was out of this world, and knew about my collection. I tried to hide it from her but she waited until I fell asleep or left the house to search for my candy. I would have shared it with her, but I was making money, and her fixations cut into my profit margin.

Mom even kept tabs on the goods I raked in on Halloween night. She followed me up and down the street on her bicycle, to monitor my progress. Kids threw eggs, bottles, and rocks at passing cars on Halloween night, but no one ever tried anything on Mom. They knew if they messed with "That Crazy Bicycle Lady," there would be hell to pay.

In the third grade, knowing Mom was on the prowl, I took all of my Halloween candy to school for a quick sale. My teacher and the principal had already warned me about what would happen if I was caught peddling candy in the hallways, so I took my operation underground. Only my best customers had access to a sale or barter.

On this day, I made a couple of secret deals before class and was feeling good about my profits. Suddenly, I heard commotion and laughter out in the hallway. The noise travelled like "The Wave" at a football stadium. At its height, Mom poked her head into my classroom.

My teacher was startled. "Ma'am, can I help you?"

"I need to see Howard. I believe he brought a bag of candy here with him."

I was embarrassed to see her and I definitely didn't want her to say the word "candy" in front of the teacher.

The teacher turned around to me like a shot. "Son, I know you didn't bring candy to school after what we talked about."

I quickly said, "No ma'am, I did not."

Mom piped in, "Howard, you left the house with a big bag of candy this morning. Now where is it?"

The class was in an uproar. First, they exploded at the sight of "That Crazy Bicycle Lady" at the door. Then, they went even more hysterical watching the teacher, Mom, and me going back and forth in a spat.

I tried to reel Mom in. "Mom, shhh. shhhh. Please!" But it was too late. All the ruckus drew the principal out of his office and down the hall to my classroom. The teacher told him I'd violated his orders about not bringing candy to school. Mom and I were whisked to his office to discuss my punishment. This was quickly turning into a bad, bad day.

The principal told Mom it was customary to paddle students who broke his rules. To demonstrate how serious he was, he drew his paddles out and started banging them on the furniture, just to make sure they would hold up when he bludgeoned my behind. He smashed them on top of his desk, he slapped them over his knees. Little did he know, I was shaking in my boots just from the sound of his voice.

None of the kids at school played poker with the principal. He could read anyone's cards, so we avoided him at all costs. Now, thanks to Mom, he had finally caught the elusive coyote. My head would definitely make his trophy case.

Mom picked up one of his paddles and handed it over to him. "Let him have it until I say to stop." Of course, I thought, *What the hell?!*

After three shots to my rear end I looked over at Mom, but she was staring at the ceiling and smacking her gum. Even one blow from the principal was too many. I screamed, "Ok, stop!" But Mom said nothing.

When we were at seven blows and counting, I screamed again. "Mom, tell him to stop!" Once again, she said nothing. The licks kept mounting and I yelled, "Red light, Red light! Whoa! TIMEOUT!"

Finally, she said, "I think he's had enough." But it took more than her words. The principal had zoned out to everything and everybody. His tunnel focus was strictly on beating me like a saturated welcome mat. Luckily, Mom touched his shoulder and said, "Whoa! Wait a minute, fella!"

The Principal had a look of a deranged child who had been admonished. I don't know if he was having a panic attack or if he was just hell bent on beating the snot out of me. Whatever it was, he had a scowl on his face long after Mom told him to quit. It was clear he would be on the lookout for a sequel in the near future. I could tell he wasn't going to rest until he finished me.

Next up on the deranged front, Mom said with a sneer, "Howard, how do you like your candy now? Enough to take a licking?"

After that experience, I gave up Trick-or-Treating and the candy trade altogether. Nothing was worth a beating from The Principal with Mom egging him on.

The Little Rattler

The girls at school hated me with a passion. I'm sure I presented a mental conflict for them. I was a semi-handsome kid with a shameful connection to "That Crazy Bicycle Lady." Most of them would rather beat me up than be my friend.

Stephanie was a girl all the boys admired. She was the teacher's pet and the doll of the class. She was a small and pretty thing, but mean as a rattlesnake. No one else agreed but no one else was in her line of fire the way I was. To make things worse, she got away with everything. Once, she threw a brick at me in the middle of homeroom and no one said a thing.

I caught Stephanie's fury every day from 8:00 a.m. to 4:00 p.m. Some days, I even caught her venom on the way home. She'd have her rattler friends – primarily girls – antagonize me all the way to my doorstep. Every so often, I got a blow to the back or a shove to the head from one of her pack as Stephanie kept me distracted. She was just as cunning as she was cute.

Jerry thought I had the juice because he often saw Stephanie and her serpents following me home. He was too dense to notice I wasn't in the best condition upon arrival. Usually, my shirt was torn, or I was missing a shoe, or my schoolbooks were ripped.

I don't remember tipping my hat to Stephanie, or smiling at her, or saying anything out of place. Yet, she had it in for me. Whenever the teacher left the room, kids would immediately rearrange their chairs into a circle for us to fight. It didn't matter if I was in the middle of my workbook. The sudden screeching of desks meant it was time to protect myself and come out swinging. I didn't want to hurt Stephanie but the battles took place nearly every day. Of course, I stayed in trouble because of those clashes. Stephanie did things just to prove how bad she was. She grabbed my test papers, copied my answers, then showed me our identical results after the grades came in. She tattled on me whenever she found the chance, too. For example, our teacher made us eat everything on our lunch trays regardless of our appetites. Some kids ditched the food they didn't like, and I hated cooked carrots. Stephanie always told the teacher when I threw my carrots out, which meant I was forced to eat a second helping while Stephanie and the teacher looked on. My hair was about to turn orange from the heavy consumption of cooked carrots.

The snake had to be stopped. I had to find a way to get her off my back without beating her up.

Stephanie really looked forward to Christmas just like most kids. While everyone was making their lists for Santa, I brought up 'The Big Lie'. I boldly told Stephanie Santa wasn't real. He was just a story our parents made up; not some jolly guy with a beard and a sleigh full of toys. My revelation crushed her sole.

Her tears flowed like a river when she was hit with the truth, and miraculously, my plan worked. Stephanie never threw poison my way after that. Happily, she moved away before fourth grade and I didn't have to worry about her hateful venom anymore.

Mr. Frankenstein

Only a few people had cars where I grew up. Everyone else, most famously Mom, had bicycles; everyone except my brothers and me. I started collecting scraps of used or broken down bicycles to build my own. It took a while, but eventually I got the parts I needed.

With all the mismatched pieces, I built the beast of bicycles. In fact, my bike was known all over town as Mr. Frankenstein. It was a jalopy, but it got me where I needed to go. It had different colored handlebars and off-color rims. The seat was all patched up and the tires were different sizes.

Mr. Frankenstein was such an eyesore that others kids wanted a chance to ride it. Only a select few got the chance, but Jerry and me ran all our errands to the store and back on Mr. Frankenstein.

Through my new beast bike, I got to know Mr. Oscar, who lived near Mississippi University for Women (MUW). He had his own repair shop with every type of bicycle imaginable. He had tall bikes and small ones. He had bicycles with steering wheels and bicycles with lights. It was like a museum in his garage. I'm not sure what Mr. Oscar did from Monday to Friday, but on the weekends, he was a craftsman. I used to stop by his place just to ogle at his collection and get pointers about repairs.

I'm pretty sure Mom bought her bicycle from Mr. Oscar, but I didn't dare mess with her bike. Plus, I was too embarrassed to be seen on her transportation, so I stuck with my own.

Christmas time stood out because all the kids in my neighborhood got bicycles for presents. I remember their smiles and the sounds of glee, canvassing the community like the birth of freedom. There were parades and more parades showing off their granted wishes. It was like a grand bicycle convention.

Every Christmas, I hid Mr. Frankenstein because I didn't want anyone to shame me or my ride. Mostly I stayed inside, but sometimes I went out to play The Flagman or the Traffic Cop. It was my way of getting close to what was new and hip in the bicycle world.

Tricycle Carl

When my brother Carl was only four years old, he wanted to get in on the cycle world, too. Out of sheer luck, someone from work gave Mom an old, used tricycle. Suddenly, Carl felt like he fit in. However, I hated that thing. It had a terrible squeak that was similar to the bell on a cow. We always knew where Carl was due to the noise from his tricycle. He pedaled that thing around inside the house and all over the yard. He drove me so bananas, I hid it whenever he fell asleep. Of course, mom got on me for being cruel, but I had to come up with something.

One day, I got the idea to create a contained tricycle play zone for Carl a short distance from the house. It was a solution to get some relief from his horrible squeaking tricycle. Unfortunately, my scheme bit me squarely in the butt. Mom told me to watch Carl while she went shopping at the corner market. When she left, I got Carl all set up in his new play zone on his bike, and then got busy on an imaginary game of marbles against my arch nemesis, Lu Lu, and his cronies.

Even in the third grade, Lu Lu had been a bully in training. He was a handsome kid and all the girls liked him, but he was always trying to fight me. I wanted to beat his ass so bad, but beating Lu Lu came with a side dish of extra trouble. He had cousins, brothers, and uncles around every corner. If I fought Lu Lu and won, it would be a long road ahead for little old me. I hated him even more because I could never lower the boom on him. I would have given anything to put him away, but knew all too well what would follow if I did. My only choice was to duke it out on the playground playing marbles.

So, I practiced shooting marbles all the time, and imagined my sweet victory. I was doing just that and celebrating in my Winner's Circle when suddenly I heard Carl's tricycle squeaking toward home. I was so engulfed in my game, the house could have burned down right in front of me and I wouldn't have noticed or smelled a thing. I was supposed to watch my little brother, but he slipped off to the corner market where Mom had gone. Usually, I knew where he was due to that stupid squeaking bike, but I was busy taking down my tormentor in my imagination.

At the sound of Carl's trike, I started to imagine the sticks, shoes, brooms, and belts connecting on my rear end when Mom got back. My butt whipping wasn't very far off from that vision. It was one of the worst beatings Mom ever gave me. Even though I went tone deaf to Carl's departure, I had a hard time accepting that he snuck out of his play box without me having the slightest indication.

Integration is No Match for That Crazy Bicycle Lady

In the fifth grade, my school integrated and the white kids were bussed over. Most of them were from the Palmer Home Orphanage. It was a new experience for all involved, and there were fights nearly every day. To be honest, we didn't even know why we were fighting. Most of us had never had any interaction with white people before. As the year progressed, everyone settled down and learned to get along.

Because I was constantly ridiculed and attacked, I had a skill for watching and observing people. I was amazed to see the hierarchy and brotherhood among the Palmer Home kids, even though they weren't related. Those kids supported each other like blood relatives, and they were difficult to get to know. It could have been their new atmosphere, or it could have been their "us against the world" mentality.

Around the same time as the school integration, my family moved to a shotgun house in the Red Line – a community across from Friendship Confederate Cemetery. Not too far was an apartment complex that housed only white residents. One of my new classmates, Nate, lived there. His mom dropped him off at school every day. I observed Nate as he said goodbye to his mother and gave her a kiss before he headed off to class. Those goodbye kisses blew my mind. I wasn't used to that type of affection between a parent and a child. Plus, I kinda thought he was too old for that stuff. Nonetheless, I was spellbound by their public display of affection.

Nate quickly started showing signs of becoming "the smart guy" in the fifth grade. I only allowed select kids to take that title. Even though a few other kids scored better than I did, I wasn't intimidated by them. Nate was different. He was a loner, like me, and he ate school up. I was definitely in awe of him and a little jealous, too.

Long story short, I got into a disagreement with Nate and threatened to beat him up after school. He was probably the smallest guy in our grade. I figured I'd wolf at him and he would cower down in fear.

The venue was set. After school, everyone knew there was going to be a fight at the flagpole between the two geeky kids. I got to the site first and had people holding my books. Everyone knew me as the studious guy, so this was my opportunity to get some street cred. People had seen me talking big noise and making big threats like a real badass. I thought my image would forever be changed if I was able to scare off little Nate.

But like a scene from a Western movie, that scrawny pale white kid showed up prepared to fight. I was flabbergasted. He wasn't going to back down.

I looked Nate in the face and said, "Man, I am not

going to fight you. If you're bold enough to show up here, surrounded by African American kids, then you definitely have my respect."

Believe it or not, we became best buds from that point on. We did our homework together, and I had to up my academic game because of Nate's smarts. He invited me over to play with him all the time and his mom often asked me to stay for dinner (although I never accepted). Everything was going great until Nate's mom met "That Crazy Bicycle Lady."

Nate and his mother dropped by unexpectedly one day, and their surprise appearance went very badly. Mom cursed and shouted at them for no reason whatsoever. She was always looking for a confrontation, no matter who was in her way. I was so embarrassed. Of course, she didn't care.

Nate and I never hung out again after Mom gave them a taste of her insanity. We drifted apart and it wasn't long before Nate and his mother moved away. Thanks, Mom. My first white friend and in one brief encounter, she demolished the bridge we'd built.

Losing Gloria

The summer before sixth grade, a kid named Barry Ellison moved to Columbus from Chicago, and we became friends. Even though he was about a year and a half older, we were heading into the same classes.

Barry was a unique character. We connected on many levels. He had much more life experience. I could out-wrestle bigger opponents, but Barry taught me hand movements like a boxer. With his help, I learned how to protect myself.

I stayed over at Barry's house for days on end. My mom never questioned where I was, but I felt guilty being away from my brothers. I was eating good food, sleeping comfortably, and watching all the best television shows. Barry's mother even bought me my first brand name shoes, Lew Alcindors. It was mind-blowing for me to finally have such quality shoes.

I learned about girls, fashion, and socials from Barry. It was a different time because I wasn't fighting with the street hoods as much. Barry never joked about my mom and never sided against me. He was as solid as a real brother.

The two of us became friends with our schoolmate, Gloria. Gloria was tall, cute, and sexy. If it weren't for Barry, I would never have gotten to know a charmer like her. Gloria had many admirers, mostly older guys. Of course, Barry had a thing for her too, but she kept him at arm's length.

Gloria invited us over on the weekends. We talked about everything, listened to music, and went to the movies. She taught us how to dance and she taught us about dating. She gave us a swag we badly needed. Gloria looked out for us and we looked out for her. We fell into tandem, and she was a constant friend for about two years.

One weekend, Barry and I left town with his family to Quitman, Mississippi, and abandoned Gloria for a couple of days. We promised her we would catch up on lost time when we got back. Barry and I had an amazing time on our getaway. We stayed at his aunt and uncle's house, which used to be a funeral parlor. It was very cold with few windows. There was a back room filled with leftover coffins and there were makeup stands and jars of formaldehyde for preserving the bodies. We were spooked silly from beginning to end.

As if that weren't enough, Barry's uncle told us a ghost lived there. He showed us a bullet hole in a door where Barry's aunt had tried (and failed) to shoot it. We didn't sleep a wink the whole weekend. There were constant sounds of creaky doors, slamming windows, dripping faucets, and power failures. Barry and I went into complete survival mode. We spent most of our days playing outside until we were forced to come in. We were so spooked, it was hard to eat and even harder to go to bed. Barry's aunt and uncle thought it was fun to tell us ghost stories they claimed were true before bedtime. We tried to keep each other awake from dusk until dawn. If one of us fell asleep first, we'd nudge the other awake again.

On our second night, we became hyper-alarmed when we noticed the carpet was moving. After mustering the courage to investigate, we discovered a large house rat was scurrying around the room. We practically broke down the door trying to escape.

The next day, Barry dared me to crawl into one of the caskets. I'd had many experiences in cemeteries, but this was way closer to death than I wanted to be. However, the dare came with a cash reward, so I took him up on the challenge. I was getting bolder by the day.

At the corner market in Quitman, I noticed some refrigerator magnets that were shaped like little voodoo dolls. They would make a nice little souvenir of my visit to this haunted place. I couldn't wait to show off my purchases when I got back to Barry's aunt and uncle's house. When I pulled out the voodoo doll magnets, everyone dashed out of the room as if I held a skunk in my hands. Later, I was forced to burn the magnets, gather the ashes, and bury the remains away from the house. I guess voodoo dolls were the kiss of death in those parts.

As strange as our weekend was, tragedy struck at home. When we got back to Columbus, we learned that Gloria had drowned while swimming with some of her older teenage friends. The news was so shocking; Barry and I never even talked about it. We couldn't go to her burial service. It was too hard for us to handle that Gloria was gone. We had all been so close.

I don't know why, but I couldn't face Barry after we lost Gloria. I felt guilty for not being there to protect her. I felt guilty for having so much fun over the weekend when she needed us. I felt guilty that maybe the voodoo dolls had brought about her untimely death. I was ashamed and numb.

Barry and I eventfully found new friends and grew apart, but he and Gloria were by far the best boyhood friends I ever had.

PART IV:
BOYHOOD:
BASEBALL, BULLIES,
AND THE BAPTIST CHURCH

Pray and Pray Some More

D ylan was completely swept away by my stories from so long ago. The one about Gloria made an impact. He grumbled, "Man, that's a tough one. I'm sorry you had to go through that. Sounds like your childhood was rough."

He signaled to the beach waiter for another drink, and took me, once again, back to the bombing in Afghanistan. "How'd you get out of that dining hall? Did you ever reconnect with your friends?"

I explained to him that as I stood in the exit doorway of the dining hall and considered my next move, I worked the "Prayer Line" like a newborn Christian. I prayed for all of us. Thank goodness the receiver wasn't off the hook. I confessed and made promises I could never live up to.

I had to get back to the dorms and the Safe Room. I whispered another silent prayer. "Please God, if I get out of this alive, I swear to atone for past sins. I'll be a better brother, nephew, son. Please get me to safety."

Blood rushed to my head so fast, I had to stop and pull myself together. Driven by sheer adrenaline, I made a Hail Mary dash to the dorms. I was getting closer to shelter but it seemed like miles away.

My room was on the second floor, across from the Safe Room. I needed to climb the stairs to survive. I made it to the steps, but stopped before ascending. The stairwell was dark, empty, and deathly silent. Ever so gingerly, I crept through the dark, alert to any warning sounds of oncoming killers. I heard nothing, and pushed onward.

Upstairs, many of my contractor colleagues were laid out on the floor in various states of disarray. Most of their injuries were scrapes and deep cuts from the explosion. Everyone was in a daze. No one looked normal and no one spoke. I had made it to the shelter, but I still felt vulnerable and cold.

The people on the floor were all somebody to someone: a father, a mother, friend, son, daughter, husband, wife, teammate, colleague, brother, sister. How had we gotten ourselves into this mess? What events from our respective pasts had led us to this triage?

As I stared down the hallway of the wounded in my memory, my mind again hurtled back in time. I thought about Mississippi and my mom. I thought about baseball, bullies, and the Baptist church.

Dylan gave me a nod, topped off my drink, and back down the rabbit hole we went.

Remember My Name

My best friend, Hill Harris, talked me into playing organized baseball at the age of ten. He was on a local team sponsored by KFC. I thought it couldn't be much different from stickball. Boy, was I wrong.

I sucked at baseball. I was the worst player on the squad, if not in the entire league, which had about twelve teams. Since the squad was short of players, I got to participate even though my skills were pure comedy (to everyone except my teammates). The coach placed me in right field hoping I'd never see any action. When a ball did appear, the coach's fears were realized. I'd drop the ball or boot it badly. When I was at bat, the coach ordered me to squat to decrease my strike zone. I couldn't hit a ball if you held it right in front of my face and it looked like a Big Mac. I was a complete disaster. The only thing that made me stick it out was my friendship with Hill Harris. Plus, I had nothing better to do.

At the end of the second season, it was obvious that no one wanted me back the following year. I took offense at being the laughing stock of the league; I was determined to get better and prove I had it in me to be a good player.

During the off season, I got Jerry to work me out as much as possible. Every day, I begged him to pitch to me again and again until he couldn't stand it anymore. I was going to matter in that league. I was going to get my redemption when the new season started. I didn't even think about quitting.

When we moved to another section of town, I started working out with the local team, U.M. Baptist Church. The coaches made a deal for my trade. The new crew couldn't believe their luck of receiving such talent and my old squad felt even more fortunate to rid themselves of the team weakest link. Those off-season practice sessions with Jerry had paid off, and I couldn't wait to restore my image.

On opening day, we were slotted to play the late game, right after my former team. Laughs and jokes ensued when my ex-colleagues saw me on the field; they were so relieved I wasn't playing with them anymore. But rumors started to swirl that I wasn't the same player I had been the year before. Yet, none of the guys in my previous unit were buying it.

When our game began, I slowly marched out to the shortstop position. The shortstop is essentially the quarterback of the infield. It's dead center to all the major action. I was "the operator" now, not the guy hidden away in right field. I heard my old teammates snickering and joking. They stuck around to laugh at my performance, now that it no longer affected them.

It didn't take long to assert myself. I was diving after would-be singles and made them outs. I was rushing bunts and gunning down runners. My batting was stellar. Then, I took to the mound to close out our victory. Before the game was over, my ex-coach was fighting with my new coach. He thought he'd been suckered into trading me away.

It was a moment I've sealed into my memory forever. I walked away from that game with a huge smile on my face. I had proven so many people wrong, and I overcame the distinction of being the worst baseball player in the league. It was an accomplishment that launched my self-confidence and inspired me to practice, practice, practice. I was the one laughing now.

That's My Boy

As a preschooler, I had picked up on conversations between Mom and Aunt Kathy about my dad. Of course, there were a lot of kids without fathers in my community, but it was a weird thing for me. I was used to the madness of Mom and Aunt Kathy, so the thought of someone else having authority in my life was frightening. I sorely needed discipline, direction, and a role model, but I was afraid of another insane parent. I only wanted a level-headed dad.

I listened to other kids idolize their stray fathers. They spoke proudly about meeting their dads and even bragged about the restrictions their dads placed on them. It was their way of letting everyone know they actually had a father. I didn't see the glamour in it. I accepted that I was fatherless, just like I accepted that I was poor. When asked, I simply said that God was my father.

Like any rebellious child, I loved the fact that I could do whatever I wanted, whenever I wanted. I came to cherish the freedom of being able to come and go as I pleased. Still, I hated the reality that I had no support and no love. I was at an age where I really needed a reliable voice to talk to. I needed a mentor in the worst way.

Here's the thing. In my whole life, I never asked Mom or Aunt Kathy, "Who is my dad? What can you tell me about him?" Even though I hadn't met him, I just happened to pick up who he was at an early age.

When I was nine years old, I saw my real dad at a local grocery store called The Little Star. Up until then, I had no idea what he looked like. I only knew his name. At the grocery store that day, I heard someone address a very tall, good-looking man by my father's name. Chills ran down my body like electricity. He was a giant compared to the miniature-sized kid I was.

I didn't know him and he didn't know me, but I felt intimidated. I could tell he was someone important and unlike anyone I knew, except maybe the pastor or the school principal. I purposely walked as close as I could in order to get a good look at my father, yet I was too scared to say anything.

Coincidentally, my baseball team just happened to be sponsored by my dad's church, U.M. Baptist. The team had existed long before I picked up a bat and glove. I remember saying to myself I would set the ballpark on fire if I thought my dad was watching.

Not soon after, the potential of playing in front of him came to pass. After a successful season on the U.M. Baptists team, I was selected to rejoin my old KFC team. We were in the playoffs against the Northside champions and the game was scheduled on a field across from my dad's house.

Did he know who I was? I doubted it. Would he be

at the game? I wasn't sure. But I planned to bring my A Game.

When I got to the park, I was shaking like a leaf on a tree. There had to be a thousand people in the stands. It felt like they were all there to critique me. I was as scared as I had been when I first started playing baseball.

In that game, I was the starting second baseman. I was expected to be a major link to the team's chance of victory, but my focus was off long before I took the field. I watched the crowd instead of the game. When play began, I made the first error on a routine grounder that cost us two runs. We were getting our hats handed to us. I wasn't even close to playing at my normal level.

I had to pull myself together. I was always a tough out in the Southside league; I had only fanned out five times that whole season. Three of those strike-outs were due to silliness on my part. On this day, I faced the toughest pitcher I had batted against all season, yet he wasn't even the opposing team's best thrower. They were loaded with talent beyond anything I had ever competed against.

We were down six to zero in the fifth inning when we got two players on base. It was my turn at bat. I knew it was time to deliver the goods or forever live in shame. Like magic, I hit a line drive that came within inches of clearing the right field fence. The shot brought all the runners home, and I landed safely at second base. I had never homered in my brief career but that moment felt like a Grand Slam.

Eventually, I scored through a steal. I had a hand in all three of our runs. Even though we lost the championship, I felt like a weight had been lifted. Our team only had two hits for the entire game, but my two-run double was the biggest. It was also the farthest hit for either team.

I may not have made my dad proud that day, but I was happy, and I didn't have to leave the park with my head down.

To Market, To Market

I took my exploits from the ballpark to bed when I got home that night and relived my performance in my sleep. The gorgeous Jane Kennedy was doing the follow-up interview. I knew I had played well, but Jane Kennedy! Wow! She never covered baseball, so this was a Special Edition featuring yours truly. I was smiling from ear to ear and waving at the camera with my eye brows.

As Jane started to talk, I grew more and more dismayed with the interview. Instead of asking about baseball, she kept asking about dead dogs and haints. "How do you howl against the wall without a body? What are you doing in my house? Hey dogs, who sent you?"

I looked at Jane with confusion and consternation. I looked over to the cameraman. I stared into the crowd. What was going on here? This was getting out of hand.

I woke up abruptly to Mom in one of her zones. She was ripping with pure madness and screaming, "Do you have something to say, you devil ass dogs? I see you! You come up in here and disturb me! Ha ha, Ha ha! Not me, you worthless dog!" She went back and forth with the wall, running from room to room, imploring the ghosts to take her on.

Jerry was at Aunt Kathy's house and Carl could sleep through a fire drill, but it was time to get him up for school. Carl always cried when he was woken up, but I needed to get the little man prepared. Plus, I needed teamwork to break Mom's spell. She was in overdrive, and it wasn't wise for me to go it alone and risk her wrath. Mom was known to attack if anyone tried to interrupt her episodes of rage. Carl was only six years old, and I knew Mom would not react as fiercely toward him as she would a solo idiot like me.

After Carl dried his eyes from being woken, I said, "You need to help me with Mom."

"Okay," he said. I grabbed Carl by the hand so we were a unified force, and to make sure he didn't back out.

I asked Mom, "Aren't you going to be late for work?" Carl joined in, "Yeah Mom, you're going to be late!" She took her cue and the spell was broken. She stopped her charade, grabbed her purse, and out the door she went.

Phew. Now, at least I could hear myself think. I wanted to make breakfast for Carl, but a mouse had tunneled a hole through the loaf of bread. We only had a few slices of bologna left. Mom was out of Food Stamps, and we were out of luck. Her welfare package was due to arrive the following day and we could restock. Carl and I had to make sure mom bought groceries when the supplements arrived.

Going to the grocery store was always complete chaos. I never passed up an opportunity to show off my throwing arm, so Carl and me wasted no time playing catch with the paper towels on display. Carl moved to avoid the buggies and other customers, ducking them like linebackers.

As raucous as Carl and I were, Mom was a one woman wrecking crew. She went into full bumper-car mode with the other shopping carts and anyone who stood in her way. She rammed them as if they weren't there at all. Nothing and nobody would impede her progression around the store.

Carl and I only went along to ensure Mom bought real food, because she loved sweets. She bought tons and tons of junk food we didn't want to eat anymore. Our bodies had started rejecting the stuff. So, when Mom grabbed four or five bags of cookies, I tried to distract her as Carl put three packages back on the shelf. This routine went on for virtually every item she placed in the cart until Mom caught on.

When she figured out what we were up to, she threatened to knock the hell out of me with some canned goods. Then, she shifted into her zaniness. When other shoppers left their carts unattended, Mom took things out of their baskets or threw in items she had reconsidered. She had no remorse about it.

I was the turncoat on our team. When Mom wasn't looking, I replaced her cheap or no-frill goods with better name brands; a trick that rarely worked. Mom bought breakfast cereal that became too soggy for consumption when milk was added, cheese puffs that stuck to the roof of your mouth, bologna that came alive when placed on a hot stove, bathroom tissue that slid off your butt like a wax job, and bug spray that made the night crawlers greet you with a smile.

The chaos continued at the checkout counter, where Carl and I desperately tried to get our quality goods through. Mom cast aside anything she hadn't selected. She threw the things we'd snuck into the cart back at us and said, "Take this mess back, and this mess, and this! Do I have to beat the hell out of y'all?"

Then, the other customers complained about the foreign items in their carts. Most of them knew it was "That Crazy Bicycle Lady" who annihilated their shopping baskets. Everyone squabbled and accused Mom of wrong-doing.

"Lady, you took my loaf of bread."

"Lady, where's my peanut butter?

As expected, Mom fired back. "I will put this jar of mayonnaise on your head! Don't let those dogs get in! You just keep your basket away from mine!" The clerks and security guards had to step in.

Finally, we were on our way with pound cake, cookies, candy corns, and ice cream. We were looking at another week without any real food.

Give Me that Old Time Religion

Baseball had my interest, but Mom and Aunt Kathy had other plans for me. In the Baptist South, children have to commit their life to Christ between the ages of ten through twelve. Jerry went through the process, which was called Revival at our church, at thirteen years old. He was allowed to put it off until that age because he was, well, Jerry, but Aunt Kathy was not about to let me go beyond the normal age before I got baptized.

The baptism process started with abstaining from television, sports, and secular music for two weeks. I had to stop playing baseball right when I was making a name for myself. The toughest part was that our church was only a block away from the ballpark. I could hear the cheers and the commotion loudly from the church grounds. I was not a happy camper. Yet, I had no choice in the matter. My team even started to struggle while I was on my sabbatical.

During the two weeks of abstinence, kids were expected to pray and ask Jesus for salvation. It was believed in my church that salvation included being touched by the Holy Spirit, which was evidenced in one of three ways.

One: Witnessed by a relative, while the candidate was at home in meditation. The relative needed to be a well-respected member of the church.

Two: A show of raw emotion during Revival service. This was the Gold Standard for salvation. The congregation lived for a fiery confirmation of faith. It appeared to be the sole reason members attended night after night. Kids sang, danced, cried, and screamed when they were touched by the Holy Spirit. The Faithfuls jumped at the chance to be seen escorting an emotional candidate to the pastor's pulpit. That move gave the members a lot of Church credibility as being committed to Beacon Central and The Spirit of the Lord.

Three: The Walk of Faith, which was just a show of confidence. It was an implied statement that said, "I'm a Christian and I know it."

The Summer Revival was such a big event that Beacon Central could have sold tickets and still would have had members standing in doorways. I had gone from being ridiculed in sports to being questioned about my faith. I felt all of The Southside was there to expose me.

When Jerry went through the process, he got up from prayer and started to dance and cry until Aunt Kathy escorted him to the pulpit, signaling he was ready for baptism. So, I knew how the process was supposed to play out.

Revival was a chance for kids to redirect their lives. Our past misdeeds were forgiven when we repented our sins and accepted Jesus Christ as our Lord and Savior.

It took three days before I became full of emotion for the Holy Spirit. Suddenly, I started to scream and dance. I shouted, "YES Jesus, YES!" Again and again, I cried out, "It's you, Lord! It's YOU!" I twisted and danced for what seemed to be somewhere between five minutes and eternity.

No one, and I mean no one, even dared to come to escort me to the pastor's pulpit – not Aunt Kathy and not Mom. When the service ended for the evening, I was left standing all alone. I walked home by myself feeling the cold sting of rejection. I couldn't even walk by the ballpark because I felt so low. I asked myself, "Do I need to break dance or moon walk in order to get escorted? Why was I left out there to embarrass myself?"

As I got closer to home, I remembered the three options: witness by a relative, physical escort by a member, or the Walk of Faith. No one would value Mom's confirmation if she agreed to bear witness, so she was not a good option. Obviously, Aunt Kathy couldn't be relied on to escort me. My only option was the Walk. That was it! I needed to walk myself to the pulpit.

So, I planned it all out. I would wait until the other kids were down in prayer. Then, I would get up and walk myself to the pulpit, which is just what I did. When the kids stood up from prayer, I was on the Big Stage staring down at them. I wanted to smile, but everyone—especially the older Christians—took those moments very seriously. I had to shield my happiness, but my plan worked.

All Christians can tell you the day they found Salvation. As for me, I found it on a Wednesday night, but I WALKED on a Thursday. Those two days will forever be my Stamp with The Lord.

I was baptized in the name of "The Father, the Son, and the Holy Ghost" by Pastor Keith. I was excited because the end was near. The last step was Communion later that same evening, and then I could finally return to baseball.

As the time drew near, my stomach was a wreck. I must have eaten something that didn't agree with me, but I didn't recall Aunt Kathy dropping off any food that day. I was still determined to get that revival thing behind me.

Pastor Keith led the church in Communion. Just as Jesus said in the Bible, "Take this bread as it is my body." I bit down on a small cracker. I felt sick, but I was able to stomach it.

Next, Pastor Keith said, "Drink this wine, for it is my blood." When I tried to swallow the wine, I vomited it right back up like a baby stuffed with sour milk. I really flooded the place. For that moment, I felt remorseful on the inside. It was as if God had sent me a message of shame for me not showing humility.

As Mom escorted me out of the church, I heard my detractors say, "I told you that boy didn't have the Holy Spirit! You know he's The Devil's Child!".... Most importantly, I was back on the baseball field the next day.

Sheer Madness

In the South, everyone became a Christian on Sundays. It felt almost as if we were being monitored. Gospel music poured out of nearly every house and apartment. The streets were unusually quiet. Most of the stores were closed. It was a day of respect, reflection, and worship. Curses were few and fights were rare.

Even Mom was more subdued on Sundays. She still fought with the walls for hours, but she kept it to a whisper. I couldn't help but watch and wonder what the walls said back to her.

After taking all I could stand of watching Mom, it was time to get ready for church. We didn't have any clothes worth mentioning, except for our church clothes. Aunt Kathy made sure we had "Sunday attire" because we had to look good around her friends and prayer partners. Our appearance Monday through Saturday was Mom's problem (and Mom didn't give a damn about our clothes).

Going to church gave me a good sense of flair. I judged my appearance against everyone else and got a lot of ideas from seeing the people in the congregation all duded up. I saw what looks worked and what looked ridiculous. Of course, Pastor Keith was always a fashion icon on display. He set the pace for a style I came to adopt.

I always got dressed first and then helped Carl get ready. The biggest challenge with him was his hair, which was some of the roughest hair ever. He broke comb after comb. The only combs I could get through his hair were made of metal. Still though, he wriggled and twisted, making an already hard job even harder. I teased him while I was working on his hair. "Ping pow! Ping pow! Ugh ouch! Ugh ouch!" Of course, he didn't like it, but he always teased me when he had the chance as well. After battling with Carl's hair, we put on our phony clip-on ties and were ready for service.

Walking to church was a Sunday ritual. We left at the same time and took the same path every weekend. Even the people who didn't attend church were in their same places, sitting on the same porches, or working in the same garages every Sunday.

Just before we left the house, Mom pulled out three umbrellas for protection from the blaring hot Mississippi sun. A lot of people carried umbrellas for this reason, but we were the only fools who carried umbrellas made from clear plastic, which offered zero protection from the rays. In fact, Carl and I cooked under those things.

Mom led our procession to church. She carried her big clear parasol over her head. Carl and I followed her like little ducklings with our smaller sheer umbrellas. Mom always picked the longest route to make sure we got all the attention that was possible for her walking circus. At first, we were too stupid to buck against her antics.

I have to admit, it was funny to see each other dripping in sweat, holding our ridiculous see-through protection. It didn't take long for me to rebel against Mom's walking festival and persuade Carl to get out of the duckling line-up with me. From that point on, he and I left before she was ready, so we could beat Mom to church without having to endure her sheer madness.

Center Stage

We usually arrived at church a little after the service started. I like to say we were late, but Mom probably planned it that way. She was a master at getting attention. Aunt Kathy demanded our presence, but it always came with a price. Church was mom's Center Stage no matter what anyone said. She treated the other parishioners like extras in her performance.

Mom's favorite day was Communion Sunday, when everyone broke bread and drank wine. The ushers sent trays through the pews with the exact number of glasses for each participating member. Mom wasn't a big drinker, but she took as many glasses as she possibly could just to throw the ceremony off. She downed four to five shot glasses of wine and left our neighbors empty handed. Then, she gave them a deadpan look as if to say, "Go ahead and use the empty glasses anyway!" The boisterous discontent that ensued was exactly what Mom intended.

She didn't stop there. Just as Pastor Keith began his sermon, she got up loudly to use the restroom. Sometimes Pastor Keith addressed her exit. "We're going to let Ms. Liza take her break now." Mom always returned through a door Pastor Keith least expected.

Sometimes, she even slid through the choir for maximum attention.

Back at her seat, Mom smacked her chewing gum like a four year old. She had a trick that made it pop loudly as she was chewing. (I tried for years to pull off that trick, but had no luck.)

Pastor Keith tried to ignore her. "God told Moses to go to the mountain." Then, a loud POP interrupted him. He was thrown off his game for a moment, but recovered quickly. "He didn't tell Moses to take his time. He didn't tell Moses to ask questions." POP! POP! This routine went on for most of his sermon.

Right before Pastor Keith gave his thundering finale, Mom loudly told us to get up and leave. As we marched out the door, she said, "Those dead dogs are howling in here! Go ahead, you old haints!"

The congregation rustled and whispered in disbelief, even though it was Mom's norm. Pastor Keith tried to regain control. "The Lord is moving in, Ms. Liza," he said as we left the church. But Mom had a ghoulish expression and the crowd didn't buy anything having to do with her and the Lord.

The Apprentice

Sometimes I liked church, but mostly I hated it. I don't have anything against religion, but the setup made me uncomfortable. There was a hierarchy in church. If you were nobody in the community, your status followed you to service. The only way out was to become an athlete, a minister, or a teacher.

Even though my baseball game had improved, the athletic thing wasn't going to happen for me on the level I had wanted it to. So, Aunt Kathy tried to push me into becoming a preacher. Sure, I could memorize and regurgitate information, but I didn't need anyone following me to hell. I was twelve years old and had my sights on a different position in the church. There was a desk with a bell used to signal the end of Sunday school class. I wanted to sit at that desk and ring the bell for announcements. I would go, Ding-Dong, "The Scotts family just came in!" Ding Dong, "Sister Louise has a visitor!" Ding Dong, "Deacon Smith has a confession!" Ding Dong, "Pastor Keith needs an Amen. Give that Pastor a big Amen!" Too bad that position was never offered to me. Instead, I sat silently in the pews and observed all that came together at the core of our Sunday ritual.

When Aunt Kathy wasn't singing in the choir, she sat in the same spot every Sunday. I always knew where to find her, and trust me, I had to know if I was in her line of sight. If I timed my arrival right, I was lucky to get a seat shielded by the Big Hat Sisters. It was always hard to see around them, and they were robotic with their movements. Nothing ever excited them. They worked their hand-held fans deliberately even though our sanctuary was nice and cool. They did this as a way to draw attention to themselves while appearing to be above everyone else.

Mom tried to get in on the Big Hat Sisters' act, but she was never part of their club. She didn't have the grace to pull it off like the originals. Mom fanned herself much too swiftly and smacked her gum the whole time. She pivoted like a bobble head doll compared to the methodical movements of the Big Hat Sisters. Plus, Mom's Big Hat was made of straw and covered with roadside flowers; whereas, the other ladies' hats were made of colorful artificial fruit salads.

Mom was only able to out-maneuver the Big Hat Sisters in one area. When a member was overcome by the Holy Spirit, The Big Hat Sisters veered slowly out of the way so the ushers could assist the high-spirited parishioner over to Pastor Keith. Well, not Mom. She just sat there motionless while ignoring the enthusiasm and excitement all around her. She even said to the ushers, "Take that mess someplace else!" Mom's statements or antics caused a major delay for emotional assistance from the ushers. Many times, church came to a standstill because of Mom's lack of protocol.

Pastor Keith worked the crowd into a frenzy whenever someone was moved by the Holy Spirit. People jumped up, shouted, and danced, but not Mom. I knew Pastor Keith couldn't move Mom to the Holy Spirit. I'm not saying she was never touched by the Word. I'm just saying Mom only displayed public emotion when she was pushing her own agenda.

Once, Pastor Keith called Mom out in the middle of his sermon. Mom took over by saying, "Is that the best you got, Pastor Keith? You need to come correct because I'm surrounded by dead dogs, ghosts, devils, and haints!" The Pastor said, "Ms. Liza, my book of Luke 17:6 tells me with the faith of a mustard seed, all things are possible. If you believe with me Ms. Liza, then He will rid you of those demons!"

Mom fired back at Pastor Keith, "My faith is as strong as a coconut! You hear me? A coconut! But sister Banana Head Beulah must have the hot sauce and the relish to go along with her mustard seeds! Her man, Deacon Edwards, keeps parking in my yard and making daily sandwiches at Banana Head Beulah's house!" The crowd shuffled in shock because Deacon Edwards' wife was sitting amongst The Big Hat Sisters. No doubt, Pastor Keith had gone where few dared to tread.

As his apprentice, I jumped up to cover for Pastor Keith and immediately started speaking in tongues. I knew how to leapfrog the church past Mom's outburst. I yelled, "La La La La, Ya Ya Ya Ya, Ba Ba Ba Ba, La La La La!" and rolled my eyes before stumbling to the floor. Then, I came up dancing. Without hesitation, Aunt Kathy joined me with stomps and shouts throughout the aisles. She led the crowd with, "Thank you, Jesus. Oh Lord! Oh Lord! Thank you, Jesus!"

Pastor Keith was so proud of me for having his back when Mom tried to suck all the holiness out of the church. He even tried to elevate me to Associate Minister, but I didn't want that position, either. The only role I longed for was to be a normal kid with a normal mom.

Dead Eye Red

I was eleven years old when my friends and I started to talk openly about girls. Growing up in the hood put us closer to the bad apples than kids should be. We heard all the cuss words and demented propositions. Some people lived for those moments, I happened to notice.

There was no bigger showstopper in our neighborhood than a lady called Dead Eye Red. It's been more than forty-five years, but my ears still burn with the thundering crescendo chants of "Red, Red, Red" by the men at our local juke joint. I never knew her real name, but she was the talk of the tavern. If Dead Eye Red was in the house, the place belonged to her. She headed straight to the center of the room to sing, dance, and work the crowd.

She wore a red wig that made her look like an animal in heat, and she had a lazy right eye. You could never tell if she was looking at you or looking away from you. That's how she got the nickname "Dead Eye Red." She wasn't much to look at, but she was what we called "Slim Sexy" with a tight little butt. Her body and her seductive behavior kept all eyes peeled her way, even the women.

Just in case you weren't paying attention, she would give a loud broadcast and yell, "Here it goes!

Here it goes!" Her announcement was followed with her shaking her rump like a paint mixer. Then she would ask the crowd, "Did y'all see it? Did y'all see it?" People responded with, "Go ahead, Red! Go ahead! Shake that thang!"

Her demand to be the center of attention caught the gaze of all the young perverts, too. We forgot all about our promises of marriage to Nichelle Nichols, Angela Davis, Pamela Greer, Jayne Kennedy, and Lola Falana.

Mind you, we had no business being around Dead Eye Red or a tavern, but she was way too entertaining to stay away. The tavern was off limits at night, so we could only watch and listen from across the street. But during the day, we went in for potato chips, pops, pinball, and billiards. We gave any and every excuse to get near the bar and see her show. If Dead Eye Red was there, it was worth it.

She was more than a handful; a chain smoker who drank far more than she should have. If her mouth was open, she was swearing. But music, liquor, and men revved her up like a steel locomotive. All the men, single and married, lined up to dance with her. There were fights and shouting matches just for a chance to be near her. Dead Eye Red loved every minute of it, and spanked her own little butt as she worked the floor. It was her house.

The presence of other women never slowed her down, and that was a problem. Women beat her butt weekend after weekend. She regularly had a bloody nose, a busted lip, or scratches all over her face. We often saw her folded over from being punched in the gut. Trouble didn't follow Dead Eye Red; it walked step-by-step alongside her.

To catch her at her best, you had to be there before she got drunk. Dead Eye Red wasn't too good at holding her whiskey, but she lived to drink. And she drank just to drink. Once the liquor set in, her gyrations were like a broken machine. Before long, the manager would drag her out of the bar minus her red wig. Yet, she had no shame. As soon as she was able to stand, she was back to her old tricks.

Understandably, she was periodically banned. Whenever that happened, the men stayed away too, in protest, until Dead Eye Red was allowed to return. Once her restrictions were lifted, the bar came alive again. Dead Eye Red returned to the club to mock the owners with her singing, grinding, and dancing. Her go-to song was, "I'm up in here! I'm just like a dog wagging my tail. I'm up in here!"

When I was nineteen, my friend J.B. and I were driving home from the mall on a wet winter's day and we spotted Dead Eye Red walking on the road. We turned the car around to see if she needed a lift.

Dead Eye Red never had the face of a sugar-kissed beauty queen, but time had been cruel to her. All the smoking, drinking, and late nights had taken their toll. She spoke more softly than I remembered. She even uttered a few sentences without cuss words. I assumed she had lost her wit along with her coke bottle figure.

Before she climbed into the car, I kindly let her know my back seats were very hard and very cold.

Dead Eye Red responded, "Son, when I was your age, I would sit on a seat like this and smoke would appear!"

I looked at J.B. and he looked at me. We got Dead Eye Red to her destination as fast as we could. No doubt, the old girl still had a few tricks up her sleeve.

The Mourning Bench

Our sixth grade classroom was in a trailer away from the main school building. Disobedient kids had to sit outside on a long, low bench to wait for corrective actions by the principal. The seat became known as "The Mourning Bench." In the Southern Baptist Church, the Mourning Bench was where parishioners prayed and prepared for a signal from the Holy Spirit that indicated the person had accepted Jesus Christ as their savior.

As mentioned earlier, our school principal was no one to play with. We had given him his nickname, Mr. Shell Shock, because rumor had it he'd been injured in war and left shell shocked. Today, the condition of "shell shock" is called Post Traumatic Stress Disorder (PTSD). Admittedly, we were too naive and too stupid to understand the seriousness of such a condition at the time.

No one wanted to be whipped, especially by him. It was completely useless to try to talk your way out of any ordeal, as I had witnessed first-hand when I tried to peddle my Halloween candy at school. Hell had to be a better option. We would have accepted the Easter Bunny as our Prince of Peace if it meant our rear ends would be saved. Shell Shock was the type of guy who maintained a calm demeanor and a smile as a kid launched into a lie to defend himself. Once the child crawled deep into their lie, Shell Shock snapped and brought out his paddle for a beating.

Anyone sent to The Mourning Bench was afraid for their life. Every fifty minutes or so, the principal made his rounds, to discipline those unfortunate students. Kids were always sitting out there, crying before the beatings and crying after beatings. Sounds of chaos, calamity, and despair echoed whenever Shell Shock was near.

One fateful day, I finished my test sooner than my other classmates. In my excitement, I started talking to other kids around me and generally disrupting the class. I was promptly sent outside to The Mourning Bench with the problem kids.

There were already four other kids sitting out there awaiting their fate: two girls and two boys who were at least two years older than I was. Fearing a beating from Shell Shock, I had to put together a plan of action. My clothing was too thin and too cheap to protect my skinny bones.

I talked the other kids into hiding out for twenty minutes until after Shell Shock made his disciplinary rounds. For a moment, I truly thought I was being per-suasive. I was too green to realize those four had their own ideas long before I opened my big mouth.

So, we snuck off to hide among the bushes and the trees. While in retreat, the two guys and two girls started romancing each other. Holy Cow! I was the mastermind behind this scheme, but I was quickly demoted to the lookout. The love scene alternated then went back and forth, minus yours truly. I was at a loss as to how I had drawn the short straw. Once Mr. Shell Shock made his pass, I gave the signal the coast was clear and we all went back to our classrooms with our best Oscar-winning faces.

After school, I told my classmate, Doug, about the wild scene I'd witnessed. I made him swear not to tell anyone, but he was a perpetual yarn weaver. He was determined to impress people no matter what he had to do or say. I warned him, "One slip of the tongue and we'll have to face Shell Shock. Then, neither God, nor Satan, nor the Easter Bunny can help us!" I should have known better than to trust him, but the events of the day had been too much. Like a kid at Christmas, Doug sprinted off to tell anyone and everyone he thought would listen. To my surprise, he inserted himself into the story. The way Doug told it, he and the two guys were all three romancing the two girls.

Word spread quickly. The parents of the two girls had the guys picked up and questioned for assault. The police stopped by Doug's house to nail down the final piece of the puzzle. He tried to flee, but even his mom jumped in to corral him. The poor fool was dripping in tears and screaming, "Mom, it wasn't me, it wasn't me! They are lying on me."

Thinking he was facing reform school, Doug suddenly gave a jailhouse confession. He came clean for lying and was eventually released from custody. The other boys were let go too, due to age and consent.

Luckily, I was never accused or taken in, but I went through my first (and last) initiation to being the fifth wheel – all due to a trip to The Mourning Bench.

Salvation Army Guy

When we were too little to pick out our own clothes, Mom dressed us in flashy colored duds, in all hues of the rainbow. We stood out like circus clowns no matter where we went. Even if we hung back from Mom when walking down the street, the connection was undeniable. We fooled no one. Our bright shirts, pants, and shoes said it all. The spacing was never wide enough. We were the obvious tail to her comet.

Even my youngest brother, Tommy, got the color treatment. When he was an infant, Mom dressed Tommy like a yellow and orange bumble bee. She put him in her bicycle basket like honey for delivery.

By the seventh grade, my day-to-day attire had faded badly. There was no masking it, either. Everything I wore was a hand-me-down from Jerry or a throwaway from a church donation. I tried to be creative and make my worn out stuff look fashionable, but it was a stretch.

One day after school, I was out playing sandlot football in my school clothes. Sonny Lincoln, who had quit school two years earlier, walked by and asked me if I wore the same clothes to play football as I did to school. I didn't hesitate to say, "Yes." The pants I wore were clearly too small. My gym shoes were the cheapest brand possible ("Catfish" or "Cats" for short). No teenager wanted to be caught dead in a pair of Cats, but there I was, rocking them for all to see.

I couldn't help but notice how well dressed Sonny was, even though he didn't go to school or have anywhere to be. Being that he had quit school, I didn't know how to measure the effects of Mrs. Dorothy's beating from years past. Yet, my encounter with this older Sonny planted my love for fashion. Unfortunately, at the time, there was nothing I could do about it. No money was no money.

In the winter of seventh grade, I got called to the school office. I thought, *Now what? I hope Mom hasn't stopped by to embarrass me again.* My mind was racing with possibilities, but when I got to the office, Mom wasn't there. The school counselor told me the family's house had burned down. I looked at her calmly, and said, "Really?"

Under normal circumstances, a kid would become hysterical and dissolve into tears upon learning their house had burned down. But I did not live in normal circumstances. My family had been living in a one-bedroom shack with a huge fireplace. The hearth wasn't romantic or pretty; it was our only heat source. We had a fire roaring all day and all night to stay warm, and I was constantly fetching wood in the cold and dark. If Mom was having one of her episodes or rants, she would just leave the house without putting out the fire.

The counselor was somewhat shocked by my calm response. She repeated the news, to make sure I had heard her correctly.

"Yes, I understand."

I wasn't worried about what was lost in the fire because we didn't have anything to lose. The only thing I wanted to know was if anyone was home when it happened. I was worried about my brother Tommy. The counselor told me no one was hurt.

After the house fire, I was out of school for a few days. We stayed with Aunt Kathy until Mom found another shack. I knew the fire was probably a blessing, but I had no idea to what extent. Donations started to pour in from the community and I received all new clothes from Goodwill and the Salvation Army. Those 'new' clothes made me look like a totally new person! I used my creativity to make everything look brand new. I was so happy because, at last, I could fit in.

As it turned out, the other kids hated me for my abrupt style modification. They were used to me being the bum across the room, and they were threatened and disgusted by my new look. So, day after day, I was attacked as the "Salvation Army Guy." Plus, being the kid of "That Crazy Bicycle Lady" was always a solid slam.

The Glitz Café

At one point, my mom worked at The Glitz Café in downtown Columbus, bussing tables and keeping the place clean. When they needed an extra set of hands, Mom recommended me for the job. I gladly took the position. My duties were also bussing and keeping the place clean, but I took short orders, too. I actually enjoyed that job for some time.

The owners of The Glitz Café were very nice to Mom and me. The big boss had a Studebaker sedan in perfect condition, which I ogled every day. The big boss was also the top chef. He cooked on the weekends and special days. Otherwise, during the week, I did the hamburgers, fried eggs, and toast. I gained an ear and appreciation for country music at that job; it was all they ever played on the jukebox.

The only problem was the long hours. I had money all the time, but I didn't spend it wisely. I went to the movies every weekend and splurged on fast food. It was the first time I could afford hamburgers, hotdogs, French fries, and ice cream. I had never experienced those treats outside of the free lunches at school, and it felt so good to be able to buy food whenever I wanted.

One day, I was cooking and bussing tables when I was shocked out of my shoes. A customer called me a nigger right after I delivered his food. I wasn't ignorant to the racism of the era, and I was used to bullies and their put-downs. I stood and stared at the man for a long time. I had lived in a completely African American community my entire life, and no one had ever called me a nigger before, let alone a white dude. Yes, African American people had said that word around me many times, but the sting wasn't even close to what I felt when it was directed at me. Even when Mississippi was completely segregated, I'd never been assaulted with that word.

There were so many negative thoughts running through my head. I always viewed bullies as attention getting, insecure, and devious-minded people. I couldn't help but wonder why this much older man would pick on a child. I was also thrown off because before that day, it had seemed like all the customers liked me. My meals were always delivered quickly and prepared as requested.

One of the owners witnessed the scene. She scolded the customer while I returned to the kitchen. It was obvious she knew the guy, because they were on a first name basis. It wasn't the owner's fault, but I felt so humiliated, I couldn't face her after that incident.

I really did like the owners and my job. I believe they genuinely liked me too, but being called the N word killed my joy of working there. I stopped showing up on time and eventually, I was fired for my constant tardiness. As strange as it may sound, the termination was like a release from my mental bondage. The Glitz Café had lost its glitz.

One Butt Shine Coming Up

After the Glitz Café, I only worked small jobs here and there. Luckily, I found a few hustles that brought in some money. One of my jobs was at Fred's Car Wash on Highway 82 (Main Street). I had to get up early on Saturdays to make the selected team of washers. If I made the cut, I could make $15 to $20 for the day. We serviced all the cars by hand; the more cars, the better.

One time, an old lady drove up in her shiny new Cadillac. It really didn't need cleaning, but we never turned down a customer. She said she wanted her car completely detailed and the undercarriage washed. Somewhat surprised and tickled, I said, "Ma'am, no one will ever look under your car to see if it's washed."

I really should have known better before I opened my big fat mouth. She said, "Son, no one is looking at my butt, but I wash it anyway!"

I smiled back at her and said, "One undercarriage cleaning, coming right up."

Soda Pops

The biggest of my side hustles was selling soda pops at Mississippi State football and basketball games. The university is in Starkville, which only had one soda distributor at the time. I'd get up at dawn on the weekends and walk twelve miles to get in line for selection. It would have been faster and easier to ride Mr. Frankenstein, but I wasn't confident he could make the trip one way, much less there and back every week. The bike was reliable for local excursions and errands, but that commute to Starkville was long. It was sad, because although I was the top seller at almost every game, I still had to pray I made the cut.

I got to see a lot of top athletes such as Jim Kelly, Ray Guy, Rocky Felker, and Walter Packer. I saw some big time basketball and big time entertainment, too, like The Harlem Globetrotters with Meadowlark Lemon and Curly Neal, all for free. I cared less about the games and the stars than I cared about earning the money. I could make $200 to $250 in one day alone, which was well worth getting up and walking twelve miles for. The company gave bonuses to the top seller, and that was just the motivation it took. All I needed was a formula to pull it off.

I noticed that whenever I walked directly through

the rows (especially the fraternity sections), I sold the drinks out well before I reached the other side. It turned out that people were buying my sodas just to get rid of me. They even recruited customers from nearby rows to buy too, so I wouldn't walk through their section spilling ice, syrup, and liquid all over their well-pressed outfits. Once I picked up on what was happening, it was game on! I unloaded rack after rack of sodas like hot cakes. Too bad the football team only played three home games a year.

CBS

Every guy talks about the girl next door. Mine was Clara Belle Sinclair (CBS). Her family lived two rows down from us in the Red Line community. It was the newest rural property we had moved to after the fire destroyed our home. These homes were called "Shotgun Shacks". It was said that you could fire pellets from a shotgun through the front door and the pellets would travel right out the back door without ever touching anything in the house from entry to exit.

Clara Belle was as cute as a chocolate drop. She had a smile that could make a summer day cool and a winter day warm; those smiles were for everyone except me.

Clara Belle knew about all of my offenses. I could not make any good inroads with her, nor did I try. She was something to look at, but I didn't care for the angelic little tart. I had wars to fight and bullies to reform. If I wasn't wearing my cape then I was trying to corral Mom and keep her antics in check. My schedule was far too saturated to worry about CBS's opinion of me. She hated me, with many good reasons. She had a front row seat everyday to "That Crazy Bicycle Lady"! As a matter of fact, her mother tried to get my family evicted from the Redline

Community. I was the guy to avoid at all costs. I'm sure I was on her list to beat, butcher, and bury without hesitation.

Clara Belle sneered at me whenever she saw me, and I sneered back. I had no thoughts of grandeur; I knew to leave this one alone. But even though I tried to fight it off, she grew on me, like wild grass.

Clara Belle's brothers wanted to ride Mr. Frankenstein; none of them had a bike. They watched in awe as I peddled up and down Fourth Street. When their mother wasn't home, they begged me for a ride. They had nothing to offer except friendship, but I gave in and allowed them the joy of riding my home-built bike.

Mr. Frankenstein was my icebreaker. Eventually, Clara Belle wanted to join in the fun. I was secretly excited to have something that had gotten her attention. Mr. Frankenstein wasn't just any old bike. He needed special handling. I gave Clara Belle a crash course in how to manipulate the beast, but unfortunately, she didn't follow my instructions. She drove Mr. Frankenstein right into the iron gates of Friendship Confederate Cemetery and sustained many bumps and bruises from the accident. Of course, her mom blamed me, and I became the outcast once again.

It was a whole year before Clara Belle spoke to me again. In the meantime, her mom acquired a Yorkshire Terrier that kept Clara Belle happy all the time. She named the dog Muffin. He was very cute, cuddly, and unique for our class of life. With Muffin in the picture, I didn't stand a chance of winning Clara Belle's attention.

I never did anything to hurt the dog, but I despised him. Wherever Clara Belle went, so did Muffin. She showered Muffin with food, kisses, and hugs. She ignored me like a bad cold. CBS and Muffin walked past my house day after day, and day after day, Clara said nothing. Muffin looked the other way as well. I couldn't believe I'd been outdone by a dog!

As much as Muffin was spoiled, CBS's family failed to get him housebroken, so he was forced to live outside at night. I figured if I got Muffin to like me, then Clara Belle would like me too. I snuck over and fed him after dark. He loved me during those visits, but during the day, Muffin was only out for himself. He didn't want me near his Clara Belle.

As bad luck would have it, Muffin wandered into the street one day and got hit by a car. He died a slow and painful death. Clara Belle cried for days. I had so much guilt for my jealousy and felt somewhat responsible. Clara Belle's big brown eyes stayed watery all the time. She didn't talk to anyone.

It broke my heart to see my pretty neighbor so depressed, so I jumped on Mr. Frankenstein and headed to the ritzy part of Columbus. I did lawn care for clients who had litters of gorgeous dogs none of us could afford. I figured they would work with me if I wanted a puppy. A deal was struck, and I was allowed to take one of the Yorkshire pups. I offered my free service for a whole month in exchange. The pup actually looked a lot like Muffin.

I rode over to Clara Belle's and gave her the puppy. She gave me a hug, a smile, and a scream that rattled the dead in Friendship Cemetery. Even Clara Belle's mom gave me a hug. Suddenly, I was "The Man of the Red Line Community" and I knew it. Clara Belle named the new pup Muffin as well. I called him "Muff Muffin", just to be silly. But Muff Muffin got to know me early on, unlike the dog before. I helped CBS train the dog, and we even got him housebroke. I was making incredible strides with Clara Belle and her family.

As time went by, Clara Belle shared her cola and her ice cream with me. She even let me hold Muff Muffin. Life was good. Clare Belle had seen the foolish side of me, the humble side of me, and the driven side of me. She was making my rough edges smooth. She even replaced my main fantasy girl (Pamela Grier). She was my sun and I was her moon. Just being close to Clara Belle made water taste sweeter. What could possibly go wrong?

During the summer after eighth grade, I was away doing routine yard work when Clara Belle stopped by to borrow Mr. Frankenstein. I usually walked to my jobs and left my bicycle at home, so I wasn't there when Clara Belle came by. But Mom was, and she took Clara Belle to a place my princess would never recover from.

I can't fully explain what happened, except to say that Mom was being Mom. Beyond any shadow of doubt, Mom knew Clara Belle had unlimited access to my bicycle. She had witnessed CBS joy riding on numerous occasions.

As Clara Belle approached the house, Mom asked her, "Who are you and what the hell do you want? Did those dogs send you here? Did you see those haints?"

Clara Belle said, "I came to get Mr. Frankenstein, Ma'am. Your son told me I could use his bicycle."

Mom fired back, "Why don't you ride your momma's bike? Take these dead dogs with you. Do I have to run you off?"

Clara Belle ran away in tears. She shared the ordeal with her mom.

Understandably, I was the devil boy once again— off limits at all costs. Even Muff Muffin avoided me.

A relationship that had taken four years to build was destroyed in a matter of minutes. There was no coming back after that. My Clara Belle continued to grow and blossom like a beautiful rose, but I couldn't get near her. No more shared sodas and ice cream. No more snuggles with Muff Muffin.

If life granted me three wishes, Clara Belle would have been numbers one, two, and three. Another friend lost forever because of "That Crazy Bicycle Lady."

Throwing Piss

Spot was a puppy when we got him. Actually, we didn't "get" him; he happened to follow us home. We pampered him and attempted to train him to be an attack dog. Even though we had no real knowledge of what we were doing, some of the training took. He was protective if anyone showed aggression toward us. Otherwise he was a friendly, social animal.

It didn't take long before Spot's training paid off. Jerry and I were out shooting marbles when Arthur Lewis, one of the community bullies, stopped by to pick a fight with Jerry. Without hesitation, I commanded Spot to attack him. Spot bit Arthur and ran him off.

Arthur was a fourteen-year-old thug, and he didn't take the incident lightly. With vicious revenge in his heart, Arthur Lewis snuck back over to our house that night and broke Spot's leg. We couldn't afford a veterinarian so Jerry and I made splints for his leg. Miraculously, our medical attention worked, though Spot had a slight limp afterwards.

Not long after his leg healed, Spot disappeared forever. I'm willing to bet that Arthur Lewis had everything to do with it, and I don't even want to think about what happened to our sweet Spot.

We couldn't prove that Arthur Lewis had done something unspeakable to our dog, but he was a heartless bully. Taking care of Spot was only phase one of his plan. Next, he wanted to get me for sending my dog after him. Little did he know, I was thinking about revenge as well.

Arthur stalked me and made threats on a daily basis. He would not rest until he beat me up. I knew not to go outdoors, because Arthur Lewis would surely catch me and do me in. This was a problem because we shared an outside toilet with one of our neighbors. Our shotgun shack didn't have plumbing: no hot water, no shower, and no inside bathroom. Mom and my baby brother Tommy pissed in a pot inside at night rather than braving the darkness of the outside lavatory. Once Arthur Lewis was on my tail, I started doing the same.

Lacking patience, the bully showed up at my bedroom window one night. He issued threats to rip me apart. While he ranted outside, I fetched the pot full of piss and dumped it all over his head. He shouted and swore at such a pitch and for so long, he kept all of our neighbors up until the wee hours of the morning.

Fearing retaliation, I didn't go outside for weeks. Finally, I decided to test the waters. Unfortunately, I picked the wrong day. Arthur Lewis snuck up from behind and leveled me into submission. I learned nothing from that exchange except to be more cunning and more patient in the future.

Bullies feed off of each other, especially if they are related. Arthur Lewis, Teddy Charles, and Skullhead Ned were a mini gang of cousins. They were close in age and preyed on the weak, like hyenas to road kill. Arthur Lewis and Teddy Charles were tough, but Skullhead Ned was always the instigator. He enjoyed beating the helpless more than the other two, but if one of them bullied you, the others were sure to grab a bite out of your ass as well.

Once I fell out with Arthur Lewis, I knew I was in the spin cycle for beatings from Skullhead Ned and Teddy Charles. Teddy Charles was a year older than the other two and known as the fiercest of the three.

Just like the sequel to a horror movie, Teddy Charles showed up at my bedroom window and issued similar threats to beat me into a mud-hole. He showed such rage and hatred that I feared for my destruction. He even went so far as to say he would kick the door down and beat my mom's ass as well. That convinced me that he needed a taste of the piss pot. I knew I was on the spit for two additional ass beatings no matter what I did or didn't do to Teddy Charles. Might as well give him the piss treatment.

Back in the sixties, there was a chemical called lye that Mom used to make soap. When mixed with water, lye combusted like the Drano of today. While Teddy Charles barked at my window, I asked him to stand by. Believe it or not, he actually obliged. I added lye to the household piss pot and eased it toward the window.

When he saw me in the window, Teddy Charles lunged at me with all his might. He was in my face but I greeted him with a pot full of hot boiling piss. Suddenly he screamed, "Oh Lord, Oh Lord!" He hauled ass home but I could still hear his screams of sheer terror in the distance. "Mom, Jesus! Help Me Lord! Help Me!" "Somebody Help!" "Oh God, Get Somebody!"

Once he fled the Red Line Community, I went through the same ritual of staying inside until I thought it was safe to go out again. But it's never safe when you have committed such a despicable act.

After about three weeks, I ventured out to play. All seemed okay until my playmate's eyes swelled as if he saw a werewolf behind me. It was Teddy Charles, and he was fuming with anger and fury. Quickly, I covered up in the fetal position while the blows rained down. Teddy Charles had a terrible speech impediment, and through the punches, he stuttered, "You threw wee on me! I washed my pace, I washed my pace, and it still stunk!" I couldn't help but laugh. Teddy didn't see the humor. He gave me a few more licks for good measure but he never bothered me again after that.

In this Corner

Out of boredom, hate, and stupidity, we fought a lot in my neighborhood. The gangs owned the streets and we were the underdogs. I fought with everyone: the girls, the gays, the bullies, and my brothers. The girls reacted weirdly to me; they got their kicks from punching and degrading me. The gay guys mimicked the girls: they rarely passed up an opportunity to smack me across the head. The bullies just wanted notoriety, and my brothers fought due to unchecked sibling rivalries.

Luckily, I knew when to fight and when to walk away. I secretly sized up the bullies or the newcomers in case whooping my ass was part of their path to dominance. Due to my scouting, I fought extremely well. I saw their weakness from prior battles and learned how to take them on.

One summer, my run-ins were like a neverending cold. However, I ran up the victories. Even I knew it was only a matter of time before I'd have to face a stronger opponent.

When Arthur Lewis, Teddy Charles, and Skullhead Ned promoted their protege, Boo Boo, my winning streak was in trouble. Boo Boo was two years younger but he beat up all the lightweights in the neighborhood. He was being groomed to come after me. After their urine baths, I was still high on Arthur Lewis and Teddy Charles' ass kicking list.

As a tuneup, the thugs pushed Boo Boo into a fight with my brother, Carl. I gave it a moment to see if Carl could handle himself. When Boo Boo clocked Carl too hard, I jumped him in Carl's defense. This was a pattern that would last for years.

The thugs shouted, "Now, get Howard!" I shouted back, "Yes, get Howard!" Then I rocked and rolled a battery of blows to Boo Boo's head. I chased him through Friendship Cemetery as he trampled on grave after grave trying to escape my assault. He wasn't about to get away with hurting my brother. Plus, I wanted to send a message to his promoters.

The neighborhood thugs didn't like to be upstaged. Determined to put me in my place, they showed up the next day with a bigger and tougher upstart, Boogie Bugs. This new boy was also younger, but he looked like a body builder, even at the age of ten. I couldn't believe my eyes. His muscles were rock solid! Where did they get this kid? They must have created him in a lab just to kill me.

Not only was I worried about Boogie Bugs' size; I had no intel on how to fight him. He came out of nowhere. I had my work cut out for me.

Suddenly, Skullhead Ned took stock of all the variables. He wanted to know if I was going to tell my mom about the fight.

"You bet your ass I am! She knows you thugs are after me, and I can hear her calling me now!"

Skullhead Ned went, "Nope, the fight is off. I don't want Ms. Liza looking for me!"

Amazingly, that's all it took to get me out of the butt kicking. Finally, I had survived the spin cycle of the threesome thugs—Albert Lewis, Teddy Charles, and Skullhead Ned—or so I thought at the time.

I saw Boogie Bugs a few more times after that, but we never once came to blows. Nevertheless, the Red Line Community was like a war zone. There was no shortage of menacing characters lurking around every corner, waiting to pounce.

PART V:
HIGH SCHOOL IS NOT FOR THE WEAK

Bloody Zombies

Again, Dylan pulled me back from my past to the present day. I left the bullies of the Red Line Community and readjusted my focus to the sand and surf in front of me. We were still sitting on the beach in Thailand, and Dylan wanted to know what happened after the initial shock waves from the blast in Afghanistan. I had left him in a slippery spot, having just made it from the cafeteria to the Safe Room.

Dylan said, "Man, you gotta tell me what happened next. You said your friends were lined up on the floor of the hallway. Was everyone accounted for?"

I went back to that hallway in my mind and picked up the thread.

Just as I made it to safety, I felt something wet streaming down my leg. Without realizing it, I had scraped against the twisted metal from a broken door handle and had a huge gash in my left leg. I'd been so focused on getting to the Safe Room, I hadn't noticed my injury. My heart started thumping and the next thing I knew, I was hyperventilating. I crumpled to the floor and passed out.

When I came to, I was lying on a table in the hallway as a nurse examined me from head to toe. She combed through my hair and cleared out bomb dust, glass, and paint chips. I told her about the leg wound.

She asked me to stand up and remove my pants so she could take a look. I stepped down off the table, turned toward the wall, and dropped my pants. Suddenly, the hall filled with funny catcalls and stupid remarks. We all laughed as the nurse, smiling too, evaluated my injury.

The laughter was a much needed relief for everyone who had been in a near catatonic state prior to my trouser drop. It was eerie. I watched people do a lot of unusual things. Some tried to get back to their demolished rooms for rest and relaxation. Others were mumbling quietly to themselves, and some just stared into space. I felt like a human among bloody zombies.

I asked the nurse about my leg. She said I needed stitches right away. She gave me a local anesthetic for the pain and pulled out a sewing kit that looked something like fishing gear. I tried to go to a happy place, but I was back in rewind to Mom, the bullies at home, and the crazy stuff they all pulled.

Those Dozens

The bullies loved to make jokes about Ms. Liza. "That Crazy Bicycle Lady" made it easy for them. She went everywhere on that thing. Mom rode her bicycle to work, to the market, and to school—the laughs and humiliation trailing behind her. I fought or cursed anyone who made fun of her, but the bullies' harassment was so frequent, fighting them all wasn't a viable option. There wasn't enough time in the day. I had to learn to avoid them or simply absorb the insults.

My real friends didn't take advantage of my situation or hurl jokes and silly remarks at Mom. Only a few cleared the bar. I disassociated from people, even adults, like the plague, which made me quite a loner.

Of course, kids will be kids. They played a game called "The Dozens," which was a competition to tell the funniest jokes about other kids' moms, just for laughs. Everyone wanted to get me in that game, for obvious reasons, and I always tried to duck out when the game began.

My peers knew mom was my kryptonite. No matter how high I got, they could always crash me back down to earth by bringing up Ms. Liza and her exploits. If I scored well on a test, the jokes and put-downs about Ms. Liza followed – anything to take the luster off of being a step above them. The truth,

I was smarter than all of them, even with my poor study habits.

One day, two big muscle guys named Crunch and Shank started up a game of The Dozens. Even though I didn't want in, they held me hostage and pummeled me with jokes about my mom. These were not guys I wanted to fight, so I had to go along with it.

Crunch fired shot after shot.

"If I need a spare tire, I'll call Ms. Liza."

"Hey, ask Ms. Liza if I can borrow her air pump!"

"Someone tell Ms. Liza I need a ride to school."

Everyone laughed and screamed.

Shank added,

"Ms. Liza ran me off the road."

"Ms. Liza was popping-a-wheelie!"

Crunch came back with,

"Your momma is the only lady on a bicycle to get a ticket by the traffic cop."

"I saw Ms. Liza burning rubber at the stop light."

These guys were relentless but they were scoring laughs like a pair of professional standup comedians.

Suddenly, I decided, "What the hell? I'm going after them."

I started with, "Crunch, your momma beat me to the newspaper. I made honor roll but she was put on hog patrol!"

Then, "Shank, your momma applied to modeling school and they hired her at a trailer park as a double wide."

"Crunch and Shank's moms put the mules out of business. All the farmers started using their mommas to plow the fields! After they got tractors, they put your mommas out to pasture where they finally gave birth to you two asses."

I had turned the table and the laughs were coming my way, but without warning, I started getting punches to my head and back. Crunch and Shank could dish it, but they sure couldn't take it. I had to use an emergency escape to keep my injuries to a minimum, but Crunch and Shank never tried me again in the game of The Dozens.

The Dozens Ride Again

Muhammad Ali was the one who said that talking negatively about a man's mother was cause for battle, but when it came to my mom and me, the bullies gleefully crossed that line. I have to admit, the material was unlimited. I dressed liked a bum. I lived in a shack. I had a bicycle that was more of a mule than a mode of transportation. Above all, I was the son of "That Crazy Bicycle Lady."

Even without a game of The Dozens, Carl and I teased each other just as brutally when no one was around. He called me "Little Liza." Even though I was in deep denial, I did look strikingly like her. I fired back at Carl and called him "Liza Lue," which was short for Mom's name, Eliza Louise. We tore each other apart with, "Look at Little Liza, messing up the dishes." Or, "Hey, Liza Lue is back from the store."

Our ribbing escalated to such a degree that sometimes we even went at it in front of our friends. Of course, we squashed the Liza jokes in public, but crowds gathered to watch us rib on each other. Carl lit into me with weird insults like, "Squirrel Man Howard" or "The Weed Man" or "Flower Barrel Howard, on the scene." He was always the first to get the audience riled up.

Carl's middle name was Dean, and I rode him as much as possible for that name. I fired back with,

"Sardine Carl has jokes," or, "Has anyone seen Butterbean Dean?" Then, the laughs came my way.

Carl pulled the crowd back to his side with, "Sunflower Howard and his lawn mower" or, "Mr. Sour Bread Howard, at your service." I cranked out an array of jokes to back him off. "Deli Meat Dean: The Baloney King" or, "Salmon Head Carl Dean" or, "Due Bill Dean for President." I had them rolling, but Carl was never one to quit. He would try to make me look like a country bumpkin by dropping names like, "Belvedere Hal" or, "Ham-hock Hal" or, "Boverman Howard."

My brother made me reach deep into my repertoire for a response. Since Carl had the roughest hair I'd ever tangled with, I used it against him. I called him, "Cocklebur Carl" or, "Pellet-head Carl," then finished him off with, "Dandy Dean BB Machine."

Carl and I got some comic relief out of belittling each other in private and in public, but our hearts came to a stand-still when we saw Mom going back and forth with the bullies. She was a glutton for attention, and the kids marveled at the chance to hear her spew her filth.

Mom's rage and agitation came out whenever anyone spoke to her. All anyone had to do was feed her one line and she'd go off, playing The Dozens by herself to a growing audience. Some idiot would say, "Hey, Ms. Liza" or, "Hey, Ms. Liza, how about a ride on your bicycle?" or, "Ms. Liza, your bicycle is blowing smoke."

Mom fired back with, "Don't 'hey' me. Hey to your Momma." Or, "Tell your momma to stop smoking!"

Or, "I see the dogs are howling at you and your momma. Take those dead dogs with you!" Or, "Ha ha! Where you going to run to when those dogs come to your house? What'll your momma do then?"

She went on and on, all day.

I wanted to retrieve Mom, but I was too young and scared to mess with her during one of her episodes, so, I allowed it to run its course until she got her fill. Those kids sure knew how to open Mom's box of dynamite.

Down but Not Out

One summer's day when I was around fourteen, I was sitting in the park watching the hotties pass by. This girl named Ruby Dee was in my immediate area. She had Down Syndrome, and I knew she despised me. She talked and laughed with everyone except me. On occasion, I tried to speak to her, but she just stared back or rolled her eyes as if to say, "I know you're not talking to me!" She had quite a personality.

Normally, I was quiet and reserved, but on this day, I was out for the chase. I was being flirty and the responses looked promising, or so I thought. Suddenly, a couple of guys nearby got jealous. They started teasing me about Ms. Liza. I tried to blow it off, but they were intent on breaking me. The cuties laughed and started walking away.

Now, I was embarrassed and peeved, so I gave a warning that the ass beatings were about to begin. I was determined to place my foot in someone's rear end for killing my girl game. Everyone scattered, screaming, "Ms. Liza! Ms. Liza!" The only person left within striking range was Ruby Dee.

She stepped right up to my face while everyone else watched from afar. With composure and confidence, Ruby Dee stuttered out what she came to say,

"Your mom-momma is Ms. Liza! Your mom-momma is the c-c-crazy lady who who who rides the bike!"

What a dilemma! Normally, I would punch a regular John or curse out any other Jane, but Ruby Dee was a girl with Down Syndrome. First, I wasn't about to hit any female at my mature age. And second, I would have looked like a rambling idiot to stand there and trade insults with Ruby Dee.

Instead, I locked eyes with Ruby Dee and gave her a big smile.

She was feisty and not feeling me at all. She said, "Buster, get to stepping!"

Score one for Ruby Dee. She may have had Downs, but she was not out of the insult game.

The Case of the Missing Bicycle

Every low-income neighborhood has its crooks and thieves. The Red Line was no exception. Arthur Lewis and Goat Turd were the top dogs, but Two Hands Zeke was next in line. He got his nickname because it was said if he was around, you better hold onto your belongings with both hands.

Zeke was in and out of reform school for his many failed capers. He once got caught robbing a corner market in the middle of the night all by himself. He was busted holding two rolls of bologna, but he'd hidden as much as twenty pounds of cold cuts inside his clothes.

Since I lived nearby, I became Zeke's friend by default. Most parents didn't allow their kids to associate with me because of my relationship to "That Crazy Bicycle Lady," but Zeke's mom didn't care who he hung out with. In truth, he kind of forced his friendship on me. I wanted him to leave me alone, but I was scared to say so. He even started calling me Hal.

I was afraid of Zeke for all the right reasons. He was bigger and stronger. Plus, he was a thug who really knew how to fight. He was in trouble all the time. I had to outsmart him or hide from him on many occasions.

Whenever he came to school, Zeke took my homework and my test papers just to stay afloat. I know the teachers suspected as much, but they feared him, too. The only benefit of our relationship was that the other bullies didn't mess with me when Two Hands Zeke was around.

One morning, I was in a deep sleep, dreaming about one of my fantasy girls, Lola Falana. Next thing I knew, Mom was shaking me and yelling, "Wake up! Wake up!" I thought, *Now what the hell is going on?*

Mom was frantic because her bicycle was missing. She wanted me to help look for it. I started by searching all over the neighborhood. I went in and out of the woods. I walked the railroad tracks and ravines. I found nothing. Eventually, Mom called the police to report her bicycle had been stolen.

The cops came to the house to get details, but Mom was in such a state, she didn't make any sense at all. She took those cops on a banana boat ride I'm sure they never forgot.

Mom ranted, "Those dogs took my bicycle and just stole it. Those howling bastards took my bike and went to hell. Those dead dogs bark around here without a body, and I know they are riding in hell."

The cops were so bewildered, they called a huddle among themselves. They asked the color and make of the bike. Mom shot back, "It was blue. It was a bicycle. Now it's being carried off by some dogs!" The police jumped in their cruiser and disappeared out of sight. I'd never seen Columbus's finest leave a crime scene so fast.

I knew Mom would not rest until she either found her bicycle or got a replacement. We had no money for a new one, so I knew I had to find the thing or face the worst of her episodes night in and night out. I waited until the neighborhood went dark for the evening to go out and comb the area once again.

When I passed by Two Hands Zeke's apartment, I saw someone riding away in the distance on what appeared to be Mom's bicycle. I yelled and gave chase, but whoever it was, was too far away. The person looked vaguely like Two Hands Zeke.

The next morning, I stopped over at his apartment and peered inside the window. Right there in the kitchen was Mom's stolen bicycle. I was shaking, but I knew what I had to do.

One: I had to call the cops for reinforcements.

Two: I knew Lola Falana, my fantasy date, and the whole neighborhood were watching to see what I would do. I had to settle this by giving old Two Hands an ass kicking. It wasn't going to be easy, but it had to go down.

I went to the corner market to call the cops. If I timed it right, they would swoop in to save me as I engaged Mr. Two Hands. I went back to Zeke's apartment to call him out. At the door, I knocked loudly and yelled, "Zeke, bring your sorry ass out here! You stole my mom's bicycle and the cops are on the way."

Zeke rushed to the door and said, "You did what?

I know damn well your poor skinny ass didn't call the cops on me!"

I said, "You got that wrong! They're on their way right now, you damn thief!"

Two Hands charged at me, unfurling left and right hooks that could have easily dented a steel train. I ducked them all. This guy had the hands of a brick-layer. He probably could have changed the flat of an 18-wheeler with his bare hands. The only way to come out of this alive was to keep him off balance. I had to make him pivot again and again until he was worn down by embarrassment or exhaustion or both.

A crowd started to build in the neighborhood, but no one stepped in to help me. Everyone knew I was in over my head, and they all watched to see me get my brains beat in. Zeke charged again and I met him with my best setup punch. It would have slowed a normal kid, but this guy was like a cartoon villain. He ate my punch like it was an appetizer.

I kept thinking, *Any minute now, my heroes of the Columbus Police Department will drive up and save me.* Needless to say, they took their sweet time getting to the scene. I had to deal with Zeke or get carried off in front of Lola Falana and the peanut gallery.

Suddenly, Zeke clocked my forehead with a wicked left punch and my lights went dim for a second or two. It was like I'd been hit with a sledgehammer. My eyes pulsed like a broken flashing neon sign, stating: "Hal is open. Hal is closed. Hal is open. Hal is closed." Two Hands Zeke was one powerful dude. The crowd was roaring.

When the cops finally arrived, everyone declared me the winner, even though I looked like I had been through the rinse cycle. I ended up with a broken hand, swelling above the eye, two bruised arms, a throbbing headache, and a sore shoulder.

As Two Hands was handcuffed and loaded into the cop car, he turned to me and said, "I'll be back to finish you, Hal. Don't think for one second you're not going to pay for this."

I tried to put bass in my voice and said, "You gotta be pretty crazy to steal The Crazy Lady's bike, Zeke. When she finds out it was you, you're the one who'll be finished."

Again, the crowd cheered in agreement. No one messes with Ms. Liza's bike, especially not the thug down the street.

Moving On Up, to the Projects

We moved to the new and highly desirable projects on the south side of Columbus when I was fourteen. There was a waiting list to get in and of course, Mom was at the bottom due to her low income and her antics. But, years after she applied, we finally got the nod of approval. I welcomed the much-needed change with delight.

For the first time ever, we had hot water and a shower. There were no more cracks and crevices in the walls that needed to be plugged to keep the cold out during the winter. No more chopping fire wood. No more running outside in the middle of the night to take a piss in a creepy, dark outhouse. With our move, I had a small hope of fitting in – of being viewed as less of a bum – but who was I fooling? The south side only meant that Mom had a bigger audience on a regular basis. Not surprisingly, she launched her first shot the very moment we set foot in the door.

One of our new neighbors tried to break the ice and offered us a tour of her apartment. The old lady was particularly proud of her stackable washer and dryer; features our new apartment did not have. We were excited to simply have a bathtub and a toilet, but the old lady assured us the washer/dryer was standard issue.

Mom immediately went to the manager's office to complain about her missing appliances. She accused them of being blinded by ghosts and haints. She told the manager that the dead dogs had gotten to him before she was assigned a unit. Even though she didn't make any sense, I was actually pulling for Mom this time. I'd never had a washer/dryer before.

The manager said he would look into it and off I went to school, excited about doing my own laundry when I got home. Mom rarely did our wash at the laundromat, but when she did, she mixed all the colored things with the white things. I looked like a walking rainbow or a faded stamp most of the time. But now, all this was going to change.

When I got home from school, I saw a slew of workmen going in and out of the old lady's apartment. I don't remember seeing any of their faces. All I saw were backs, arms, and asses struggling, grunting, and dragging the washer and dryer out of the old lady's home. I heard the old lady begging and screaming for the men to explain their actions. They said nothing.

As the men hauled her prized appliances away, it dawned on our neighbor that management was reacting to a complaint from the newest resident.

I stood watching the commotion until I heard the woman loudly say, "Some son-of-a-dog must have told something!" Being that I was part of her setback, I made sure to stay out of sight as much as possible. I wanted no part of her wrath.

Our management chose to rectify mom's complaint by taking this lady's appliances away. Understandably, the woman never spoke to any of us ever again.

Go Ahead Caller

In high school, like most teenage boys, I wanted to meet and talk to girls. However, if I was lucky enough to get a girl's attention, I didn't have the means or communication tools to expand upon the friendship. In other words, I needed a telephone.

Mom had no desire to communicate with anyone. Her attitude was, "I'll see you when I see you!" Since I wasn't working regularly, I had to find a way to get her on board with the idea of having a phone. After some planning, promises, and pure manipulations, she relented. Life was definitely on the upswing. I was making inroads with my social life and could talk to fellow students, running mates, and a few females.

It didn't take long for me to realize I had to time my conversations around Mom's episodes. I would be in mid-conversation with a female schoolmate, saying, "Girl, I think you're as fine as French wine," or, "Girl, you are the neckbone to my collard green," when suddenly I heard, "Go ahead, take those ghosts with you, you old devil dogs!"

If Mom appeared when I was on the phone, I ended the call immediately to prevent embarrassment. Suddenly, my, "Girl, I liked that smile today," or, "Girl, you look sweeter than cotton candy," turned into, "Let me finish my history homework and we can talk later." It was a cat and mouse game I played day after day.

Mom was as cunning as she was crazy. She always found new ways to mess with me. There I was, doing my thing, going on and on in a flow of sweet nothings – "Baby, you're like pork chops and beans," or, "Girl, I wouldn't trade you for pig's feet," or, "Bologna and bacon have nothing on you!" – before I realized Mom had pulled the phone plug out of the wall. She laughed as I used some of my best material, cooing to dead air.

Things got bad when Mom decided to use the phone herself. I came home one day to find her randomly making calls to anyone who would answer.

"Hello, who is this? Are you talking to those dead dogs? Are they at your house? We don't want them around here!" Then she'd slam the phone down and call another unsuspecting person. "Hi, is your momma home? Tell her to keep those dead dogs and haints over there! We don't have ghosts over here! Nobody gonna bang on my door. Nobody gonna bang against my walls!"

When that person hung up on her, she kept going. "How many dead dogs are over at your place? Don't send them back over here! They will howl all night!"

It appeared there was no end in sight. It was my turn to disconnect the line from the wall. Getting a telephone turned out to be a very bad idea. I quietly surrendered and accepted life without one.

At school, my classmates told stories about the

weird and spooky calls they had received the night before. Not to be outdone, I chimed right in and said I had a couple of those bizarre calls too.

Party Over Here

Back when I was selling sodas at the Mississippi State football games, I had become friends with my biggest competitor, Mauricio Garcia. He was quite the hustler, but he didn't have my sales formula. He was also great with the ladies, and I thought maybe I could gain some pointers from this guy.

The summer before senior year, my neighborhood friend, Edward Blount, threw a back-to-school party at our apartment complex. I figured if I invited Mauricio, then I could see 'the magic' up close. I asked if he was free and he said he'd be there.

No one knew Edward's party was the very first party I'd ever been invited to. There had been no birthday bashes, Christmas parties, or Sweet Sixteens for me. This would be way beyond the church socials I'd been to. I had to look Fly (clean and cool)! I had to have a Rap (smooth talk for the girls)! I had to have a Pimp Walk (slow and methodical)! Finally, I had to have Some Moves (the ability to dance and sway)! Being that I was a square (nerd), my work was cut out for me.

I went deep into my closet for my best knitted bell-bottoms. I pulled out my special nylon butterfly collar shirts. I dusted off my three-inch stack shoes. I made sure my Afro extended as wide as the crown on the Statue of Liberty.

Unfortunately, Jerry was home while I was getting prepared. Every time I walked into my bedroom from the bathroom, whatever I'd laid out to wear was gone or out of place. Jerry could not keep his paws off my spiffy duds. I ended up selecting and ironing three full ensembles.

Finally, I put my outfit on for a test run. My shirt made me look like King Arthur at the round table. My pants were special edition elephant ear bell bottoms and they flared out like the Liberty Bell. My stack shoes made me feel like I was walking the runway in a fashion show. I definitely had the Fly look down.

Next, I put on some music to work on my Rap. I got out my Barry White albums. I tried out a few lines of "*Hey Baby, What's Your Name?*" and "*Baby, Don't Be So Mean*" and lowered my voice like Mr. White with "*How About You Come Dance With Me?*" and "*Baby, You Are Sweeter Than Pigs-In-A-Blanket.*"

Then, I worked on my Pimp Walk. All the cool guys walked with a limp, so that's how I was going to walk around too. Next up were the Dance Moves, which were pretty poor. I had one or two moves but I wasn't going to win any contests. I figured I would only ask a girl to dance when the floor got crowded, so as not to draw too much attention.

Mauricio arrived at my place earlier than expected. He was more dashing and debonair than I'd ever seen him look before. At the party, he worked the girls before I could even make his introduction. But he gave me a decent plug and kept throwing my name

175

out by saying, "Hal invited me" or "Where is Hal?"

Edward and the gang took well to Mauricio. They basically rolled out the red carpet for him. He even brought cigars, which were a great prop for looking cool even though I didn't smoke.

A neighborhood showstopper, Little Awesome Annie, walked up to Mauricio and introduced herself. They quickly became two peas-in-a-pod. I was envious at first, because I had being eyeing her for quite some time, but I recalibrated quickly and tried to look cool by taking a few swigs of "Bear Cat Brew." Edward's Bear Cat Brew was a mixture of Mad-Dog 20 20 (cheap wine), Wild Irish Rose (another cheap wine), Thunderbird (cheap liquor), Annie Green Springs (cheap wine), Rum (Liquor), Colt 45 (cheap beer), and whatever he could find for good measure.

Suddenly, none other than Margaret Thunderbolt (or MT) walked in. Her name was actually Margaret Thurman, but she had a rump that looked like she had a set of twin pumpkins in her pants. The guys were pushing and shoving just to get a look at her. The room was full of sighs and exclamations of "Damn," "Wow," and "Look out now, look out!" We tried to be inconspicuous, but we were gawking like buzzards on a ledge.

Out of nowhere, Margaret approached me to say hello. I lost all pretense of swag and leapt out of my seat to offer her a drink. She smiled and accepted the offer. As I made Margaret a drink, I took a couple more swigs of the Bear Cat Brew to calm my nerves.

I never had a girlfriend or a date before. I was sweating like a pig headed to slaughter. My cool was dipping and I knew it. I puffed on my cigar to regain composure.

I couldn't believe I had Margaret Thunderbolt on my fishing line. She would be the catch of the year if I won her over. I tried to be seductive like Barry White and laid out some lines. "Oh girl, I want you to be my soda pop! Baby, baby, baby just be my sammwich!"

The lights went down and I felt a rumble and roll in my stomach. I was in trouble and I knew it. I looked for the wastebasket, but the only receptacle nearby was a dirty ashtray. I tried to release the built up saliva in my mouth and hold the rest, but to no avail. I threw-up a complete waterfall of the Bear Cat Brew, overflowing the filthy ashtray, right in front of Margaret Thunderbolt. I think I gave her some of my dinner.

People all around me shouted, "Everybody, look out! Oh, heck no! He didn't!" but mainly, "Eeewwwwwwwww!!!" Everyone was gasping, gagging, and laughing at me so hard I had to leave the party. I went home and took on the toilet while Mom battled the walls. What a disaster.

For quite some time, I was called Mr. Ashtray at school. Sometimes, the nickname was attached to gurgling noises and vomit simulations. I didn't get invited to any more parties after that.

Killer Crush

When my friend Barry Ellison moved to the North Side, I visited him on occasion, which allowed me to connect with a lot of the kids in that section of town. Those friendships served me well, especially when the South Side thugs fought the North Side thugs.

During the summer of 1977, when I was seventeen, my friends and I spent a lot of time cruising the streets while listening to music, telling jokes, and admiring the girls. Our pack was me, Rob Jones, Jerry Pharr, and Edward Blount. When darkness fell, we would split up and try to visit our girlfriends.

On a quiet evening, I dropped out of the crew and rode my bicycle over to the North Side to try my luck at romance. My girl and I decided to take a stroll around Hughes Elementary School. There were other kids hanging out there, too. The most notice-able face among them was a kid named Ronny, who was the thirteen-year-old cousin of one of my friends. Ronny was a quiet, handsome, unassuming kid. At least, that's what we thought.

Unbeknownst to us, he had a killer crush on my girlfriend. Ronny had been spying on us as we toured the school grounds. When I became aware that he was following us, I stopped and called him out. Ronny was holding a hammer-sized stick as he marched toward me. He was much smaller, so I figured I could subdue him if I had to.

Suddenly, Ronny's boyz surrounded him to halt his progression. They wanted to soothe the situation before we got into a fight, but Ronny ducked out of the crowd and disappeared. Ronny's friends knew me well, so they were making an honest effort to broker peace.

I walked my girlfriend home and wondered what had gotten into Ronny. I'd known him and his older cousin for years. I couldn't figure out what his beef was.

After I got my friend home, I was summoned back to the school to shake hands with Ronny as a gesture of goodwill. However, when I got there – eager to put this episode behind us – Ronny looked me in the eye, pulled out a knife, and said, "I'm coming for you." My mind was racing. I was afraid, but pretended to be unfazed. I wanted to diffuse the situation, but Ronny wasn't having it. I had to devise a plan to get out of harm's way.

Even though I wasn't from the North Side, I knew a few different routes to get back home. I jumped on my bicycle and made a dash for it, peddling like my life depended on it. Ronny didn't give up easily. He chased me for four long, laborious miles.

The next day I told Rob, Edward, and Jerry about my night of horror. They couldn't make sense of Ronny's aggression either.

Time passed, and one night, me and the guys were out cruising when we drove right past Ronny on the street. He was walking at a brisk pace and had a distraught look on his face. I'd seen that look many times before, on Mom's face.

I told Rob, "Hey, stop the car! There's Ronny. Let me out."

Rob said, "No, I'm not letting you out."

I was furious! This was my chance to exact my revenge. I appealed to Jerry and Edward to make Rob stop the car. They both said, "No man, let it go." What type of friends were these guys?

When I got home, I switched on the news and Ronny was all over it. He'd been arrested for shooting a guy in the area where we last saw him. Turns out, Ronny had another killer crush on a different guy's girl. Once again, the girl was four years older than him and so was her boyfriend.

When we saw Ronny on the street that night, he was still at large with his gun tucked neatly away in his pants. If Rob had let me get out of the car, Ronny would have ended me that day, just like he ended the other guy.

The Saw

I often wondered why we were never taken away from Mom and placed in foster care. Anything would have been better than the humiliation, the lack of love, and lack of attention we received. She didn't hug or kiss us. She even told us not to call her "Mom"! I learned quickly and early to hide my emotions.

I've tried to describe to my own kids how this felt. Not that I want them to be as tough as I was, but I want them to understand I lived a life with very little emotion and even less affection. I never had a shoulder to cry on. I never had someone I could lay out my fears, my doubts, or my insecurities to. Someone to tell me, "Baby, it's going to be all right." I learned to accept or resolve my own issues, and I attempted to keep moving forward.

It doesn't take a genius to realize that my brothers and I represented income to Mom. Letting go of us would have meant losing welfare money. Mom wasn't mentally equipped to mold us or push us forward. Whether she wanted to or not is something I will never know.

If I wanted to quit school in fourth grade, Mom wouldn't have said a word. The same goes for Aunt Kathy. As a matter of fact, all my brothers quit school around the ninth grade. Mom didn't take any issue

181

with it. To her, it meant she was no longer responsible for them. They could work and fend for themselves.

I was the lone holdout with school, and I became quite a problem for her. In high school, I chose not to work regularly. (It was a move that cost me dearly when I got to college and desperately needed a job. By taking myself out of the market, I had no real work history.)

The expense of a non-working, growing boy mounted day after day. The more time I spent at home, the more Mom barked and howled at the voices in her head. Her tantrums reached such a peak, I was baffled why our neighbors never called the cops. We lived in the projects and there were other families on all sides. Maybe they were afraid of her.

The last time I took matters into my own hands with her, I was seventeen years old. She was on one of her rants and I simply couldn't take another second. I grabbed Mom's homemade cymbals and percussion instruments and yelled, "Stop this crazy mess, right this second!" My adrenaline was racing, I was so irritated.

I stepped into the restroom to calm down. The house fell eerily silent, like a switch had been turned off. I thought, "Good. She's stopped her craziness. Now I can read in peace and go to bed." It was around midnight at the time, and I had school in the morning.

When I stepped out of the bathroom, Mom lunged at me with a table saw and gouged a hole the size of a quarter in my left hip. She totally blindsided me. I grimaced in pain as blood gushed down my leg; then I grabbed my coat and headed to Aunt Kathy's house for the rest of the night.

When I got over there, the only thing Aunt Kathy wanted to know was, "Where on earth did Sister get a table saw?"

And, Who Are You?

In the summer of 1977, I was at the Columbus Public Library, getting a few books, when I noticed some girls were checking me out. I started conversing with them and hoped to get lucky and win over some new friends.

Out of nowhere, a very tall man of six feet, four inches walked in. I didn't notice him approaching because I had my back to him, and I was deeply engaged in my silly conversations. The man had a shadowy presence about him. The girls knew him and he knew them. They shared warm greetings and talked about school and about books. Any other time, I would have been upset someone had disturbed my game, but this walking statue was none other than my dad!

His presence was so out of left field. In that moment, I went totally blank and lost all words. It had been eight years since I first saw him at the Little Star Grocery Store, when I had been too afraid to speak to him. I sat motionless in my seat and thought, *Oh, wow. Now what?*

It was poker face time.

My dad acknowledged me in the group and asked, "Hello, and who are you, young man?"

I forced a smile. *How do I answer this?*

No doubt, there was a pregnant pause while he waited for my response. I felt so conflicted. In one way, I wanted to remain anonymous. I also wanted to express anger for being cast aside. In the meantime, I was coming off like the cat that swallowed the canary. I had to make a decision: talk or don't talk.

I chose to reach deep within and give my introduction like a contestant on a T.V. game show. I looked my dad square in the eyes and said my first, middle, and last name. The information hit him like a punch to the chest. He stumbled and took a seat across from me. My dad sat there in utter silence while looking me up and down. I sat in silence, too.

Once he regained himself, he started to fire questions in rapid succession about Jerry (no surprise there), about my Aunt Kathy (no one can forget her), and about the mystery kid who had been scarred by boiling water (me!). I answered them all. He even asked what my intentions were after high school. There wasn't a doubt in my mind I was going to college, but I said, "I'm not sure what I am going to do." I thought it was my turn to join in the game of charades.

Without saying goodbye, he rose to his feet and walked away. I sat there, stone-faced, in shock. I asked myself, "What the hell just happened?" It felt like I had just come face to face with the ghost of myself plus thirty years.

I found my legs and walked over to the balcony. Below, I saw my dad with two cute little kids at the checkout desk. They must have been his, but it was the first I'd ever seen them. My dad glanced up at me once or twice, but when he finished helping his children with their books, he walked right out the door. I didn't know how to feel. Only one word came to mind: Abandoned.

I had a terribly lost feeling for months after that encounter. I didn't speak of that moment to anyone for many years.

PART VI:
HIGHER EDUCATION

The Wait

Dylan sat up and said, "Man, that's really harsh. I can't believe your dad was so close the whole time. And with his own little kids!"

"Yeah, there wasn't much I could do at that point. I was all torn up about it."

"Speaking of torn up, man, what happened to your leg after the blast?"

"Well, Dylan, the nurse got to work and sewed me back up. When I looked down at my thigh, there was a cornrow of twenty stitches."

I picked up the story from there.

It had been about two hours since the initial blast, and we were still in imminent danger. Surely, the Marines or the QRF (Quick Reaction Forces) knew about our predicament, but no one had been in touch with us. We had no idea if or when help might arrive.

Finally, it occurred to one of the survivors, Hayward, to do a head count. Two people were unaccounted for, so he gathered volunteers for a search party. Having just experienced a lifetime's worth of terror, I wasn't excited to participate, but I couldn't leave my coworkers in danger. I had only lived there for six months and was still a stranger in that place, but they would have done the same for me.

Before joining the search party, I went to my room across the hall to get a coat. It was 20 degrees Fahrenheit outside. The damage to my area was mild compared to others, but it still looked like a tornado had ripped through the place. I had to feel my way around because electricity had not been restored. It could be days or weeks before we were up and running again.

I hustled to catch up with the crew. Time was of the essence. Once we left the Safe Room, we were completely exposed to any and all hostilities. The Afghan guards were not the ones I was accustomed to. The original security forces had dropped their guns and fled the facility like scalded dogs.

Without question, I was scared. Even the slightest movement made me jumpy. The thought of being gunned downed weighed heavily on my mind, and I glanced skeptically at everyone I passed, especially anyone carrying a gun. I was trying to find some type of facial recognition. We were searching for our people but we didn't know who to trust in the crowd. Everything was unfamiliar, even those who had seemed familiar to us only a day before.

As hard as I tried to stick with the story about the blast, it always propelled me straight back to Mississippi and the crazy train I rode there. Dylan would just have to endure another round.

Close Enough to Touch

Before I graduated from high school, I registered for classes at Mississippi State University. Nothing and nobody was going to get in the way of me going to college, not even Mom. I figured out a way to afford the tuition through school loans and Pell grants. College was finally my chance to get off that crazy carousel! I was turning in my circus tickets.

Money from the work-study program meant I was finally able to afford my own clothes. I became quite the snazzy dresser; a blazer and khaki guy, just like the campus preppies. One day, I was browsing through jackets in a men's clothing store in East Columbus. Out of nowhere, I spotted my dad shopping in the same store. I immediately ducked out of sight through some clothing racks. I was not prepared for another sudden encounter.

When I popped out on the other side of the rack I'd cut through, there was a pretty girl with big, gorgeous eyes staring out of the store window. She had to be about thirteen years old. It was the same girl I'd seen at the library with my dad, which made her... my sister? I walked ever so near but not close enough to be noticed. I was simply curious and somewhat in awe. I wanted to speak to her, but what was there to gain? I collected myself and headed back to campus, my head spinning. This 'other' family was out of my orbit and I couldn't get clearance for lift off.

The Chosen One

In college, my friends and I partied all weekend and missed church on Sundays. Out of nowhere, we developed a guilt complex about missing services. We wrote down our respective places of worship and drew a name from a hat to choose where we would mend our ways. The winning church was New Side Baptist; our randomly selected place of redemption.

The following Sunday, we gathered in front of the church. We wanted to file in as a unit and, of course, we wanted to sit together. I was the oldest and the most savvy, so I led the way.

Since I had spent a great deal of my childhood in church, I wanted to dazzle my friends and New Side Baptist with my Christian background. I talked my guys into bringing in their own bibles. I gave them a briefing of what to expect and how we would complement all elements of the service. I assured them that our appearance would set the church on fire. I told them, "Just be ready for everyone to beg us to either join or return." As far as I was concerned, the stage was set for us to take New Side Baptist by storm.

The usher greeted us at the door and walked us to the very front of the church, where he sat us across from the minister. Our seats should have been the first clue something was unusual about our visit. We were nicely dressed—wearing blazers, ties, and hard-bottom shoes. All eyes were on us like incoming rock stars and we were eating our own hype.

I heard someone say, "get a load of those guys" as we passed through the aisles. I took it to mean the congregation was excited to see potential new members, but as we took our seats, there were sneers and looks of disgust. I couldn't wait for a hymn or a sermon; anything to get the attention off of us.

When the preacher took to the podium, he requested we stand and introduce ourselves. He started with me. I told him where I lived and where I'd previously attended church.

Out of nowhere, an old lady off to the side gave a distressful warning, "That's Ms. Liza's boy! He's the son of That Crazy Bicycle Lady!" Suddenly, there was a grumbling and rustling in the pews. I looked at the old lady and smiled in the affirmative. There were looks of concern from the parishioners, but the service continued.

My friends shared their names and previous churches, all Christian. When they finished, I was asked to remain standing. While I stood there, the pastor accused us of being the dread of Columbus.

I shook my head, "No, no!" but the crowd roared, "Go ahead now, go ahead!" The pastor lamented, "These sinners are stealing our future!"

The crowd roared back, "Take your time, pastor. Take your time!"

I looked to my friends for support, but they cast

their eyes downward and let me stand there as the sacrificial lamb. The pastor pointed his finger left and right toward our seats and said, "Here are the pushers, dope users, crack heads, meth heads, acid heads, pot heads, coke heads, and Lucy in the Sky with Diamonds heads!" This man was in a zone. There was no stopping him.

The crowd responded with a loud gasp and screams of, "Lord, help them! Lord, help them! Amen, Pastor, Amen!"

Inside, I protested, No, no! No Amen! No! but it was useless. I gave up trying to fight him off. We were his fish and his loaf of bread to feed his flock. I had no choice but to take it.

As the church service came to a close, we tried to mix in with the congregation as we exited the building. I heard one last shot of repulse directed at us, "Goddamn those backsliders!"

When we got to the parking lot, we scattered like roaches exposed to the light. Our attempt at repentance had turned into a crucifixion.

Santa Baby

In college, J.B. was my co-worker and my running buddy. I was four years older, so I treated him like a little brother, but he was good company and a good friend. He kept me laughing with his outrageous outtakes on life and relationships. I'd like to think that I was a good barrier between him and his hardships, but I wouldn't swear to it.

J.B. let me have it whenever he saw an opportunity. If I made missteps in dealing with girls—which happened often—he pounced on the chance to embarrass me. He wanted to get one over on me at all costs.

One Christmas, I bought my girlfriend a gift long before J.B. completed his shopping, so J.B. took it upon himself to try and top what I planned to give my girl. I had so much fun watching him go to store after store, trying to find something to best my gift yet stay within his price range. He finally settled on a sweater monogrammed with his girlfriend's initials. It was a very feminine garment; perfect for a girl. Admittedly, I was outdone but I wasn't jealous. I was happy for him. The sweater would surely win him good favor.

We delivered our gifts a few days before Christmas with contentment and joy. We knew we were the perfect elves for our sweethearts. But of course, J.B. wouldn't let it rest that he was the one and only Santa.

The night before Christmas, we went out partying at a club nearby. J.B. was all smiles and still giving me grief about how much better his present was than mine. At the club, I noticed J.B.'s girlfriend's brother was there. He was wearing the monogrammed sweater J.B. had given to his girlfriend! Most definitely, I was baffled as to why the brother would wear such a girly sweater, especially with someone else's initials. However, I just had to see J.B.'s reaction.

He was so shocked when I pointed the sweater out to him; he said nothing for the rest of the evening. He said nothing for days. I felt sorry for him. It was definitely a "Lord, bless his heart" moment – which in the south means "he never stood a chance" – but I couldn't stop laughing. It took weeks before I stopped bringing it up.

J.B. never teased me again. He knew I had the magic bullet to fend him off.

The Car Made Me Do It

During my freshman year at Mississippi State, I devised a plan to save some of my financial aid to buy myself a car. I made sacrifices such as borrowing books instead of buying them and eating peanut butter sandwiches instead of getting a meal ticket. With the money I scrimped (around $1,000), I bought a 1972 Ford Torino. Of course, I didn't know how to drive and couldn't afford the insurance, but Mississippi didn't require car insurance and eventually, I taught myself to drive. No one asked how I got to the DMV when I went to take the driving test, which was a lucky break for me.

Having a car opened a lot of doors. I was free to go wherever I wanted and happy to give people rides where they needed to go. MSU was only about a twenty-minute drive from Columbus, so I went home often to see old friends and check on my younger brothers.

When Jerry saw I had a car, he sparkled with excitement as if it was his car too. He always wore my clothes without asking, so he assumed he could also use my car at his leisure.

One Friday afternoon, Jerry asked if he could borrow my car. I told him sure, as long as he was back by 6:00 p.m. I had a date planned that evening. As time passed, I kept checking outside to see if he'd made it back. When he wasn't home by 7 p.m., I started pacing up and down the street.

Eleven hours later, Jerry came home. He was as drunk as a sailor on a Saturday night and I was pissed. I had missed my date and Jerry had taken the utmost advantage of me. Hysterical with anger, I demanded to know where he had been. He murmured a couple of incoherent sentences.

Spewing curses at him, I went outside to check on my car. When I turned the engine over and shifted into drive, something wasn't right. I got out to inspect and noticed that both tires were pointing outward. The tire axles were broken and the car was undrivable.

I raced back into the house and yelled at Jerry, "What have you done to my car?!"

In an accusatory tone, he replied, "I got a ticket because of your car!" Then he caught me with a sucker punch. I landed a couple of good shots back, but it was no use. He was drunk and I needed to avenge my frustrations when he was sober. It was just like him to blame my car for his foolishness.

Jerry was a bum and a mooch. Trying to get him to do right by me was like trying to squeeze water from a stone. He didn't step up and offer me any cash to get the car fixed. In fact, in an act of selfish defiance, Jerry went out a few days later and bought himself a 1970 Pontiac. He bragged that he only paid $200 for it. ($200 that would have gone a long way toward getting the Torino repaired.)

As they say, you get what you pay for. Jerry's Pontiac clunked out after just one day and I never saw it move again. I enjoyed some good laughs over that.

Eventually, I scraped the money together to get my own car fixed, but only after being without wheels for a couple of months.

Saturday Night Special

To say that I harbored an intense disdain for Jerry would be an understatement. I was still fuming about his destruction of my car, the sucker punch, and his utter disrespect for me in every way. That's just who he was; a young male version of Aunt Kathy. He bossed me and Carl around and took whatever he wanted.

I was itching for retribution for my car. Sooner or later, I knew the opportunity would present itself and I would gain some satisfaction. True to character, Jerry started a fight over something frivolous. When he came after me, I beat his butt like a busted punching bag. Jerry's long reign had come to an end.

As per usual, Jerry ran to Aunt Kathy to tattle. He said I wouldn't let him drive my car. (He left out the part that I did let him borrow it, but he had destroyed it.) He told her I beat his butt. He told her I made our youngest brother, Tommy, go to school, which was true. I thought Tommy should be in school. What's so bad about that? Still, I didn't look too good compared to her golden child.

A few weeks later, I received a visit from Aunt Kathy. I was surprised to see her because it was a Sunday morning. Aunt Kathy never missed church;

she was God's best Christian. Something sinister was going on. I could feel it.

Aunt Kathy marched straight into the living room and turned off the football game I'd been watching. She glared at me and said, "I hear you've been acting up!" I was baffled, wondering what she referred to. It had been more than a month since my skirmish with Jerry, but she made it seem like it was yesterday.

She spat out, "Who do you think you are, to come around here and put on airs? You are not to disrespect your brother! And you are not to disrespect me in this community! Plus, you're not a dad to anyone here, especially Tommy, so stop acting like it. If I have to come back here because of you, it won't be pretty!" Then, she flashed me her Saturday Night Special to show she meant business.

I sat completely mute, stunned that she would threaten me with a gun! I had never done or said anything disrespectful toward her. I had never given her lip service, or rolled my eyes, or turned a blind eye, even though she'd given plenty of cause over the years. She simply didn't take kindly to being ignored, or to anyone crossing her Jerry Boy.

Aunt Kathy was determined to show me what happened when people messed with her prize. It was in that moment, when she flashed her gun, my servitude to her ended. I was awakened like never before. At twenty years old, I finally saw the true demon in her. After that, I kept my distance more than ever.

After Aunt Kathy punked me down, Tommy quit school and joined the pack of delinquents he aspired toward. There was nothing I could do. Aunt Kathy held the gun.

Flirty Shirley

Flirty Shirley was the most voluptuous creature to ever walk the earth. Nothing can prepare you for a girl like her. Her bathwater was the appetizer and the chaser. She was as black as she was fine, and as fine as she was black. She was a pinup cast in an adolescent world. One look and you would never be the same, and she got hotter each time you saw her.

I got to know Flirty Shirley during high school. I was a student and she was a diva. She had no academic drive whatsoever. It was unlikely she'd land into any profession—not a teacher or an accountant, and certainly not a homemaker. She wasn't someone you'd feel good about bringing home to Mom or Dad. But her presence was water in a desert. Her movements were a memory. She walked through your mind and stepped on your heart. She was a tormenter and she knew it.

Flirty Shirley only dated athletes, actors, and men with money. As she said, she was only interested in "The Prime Cut." I was never her type, but we became friends. At least I was allowed to say that much, and I was delighted just to be around her. She used me and used me some more, but I was crushing so I let it happen.

In college, my car became her taxi and without question I dropped her off wherever she wanted to go. Eventually, I decided it was time to make a play and get out of 'the friend zone'. I had to take a shot at this goddess. In between shuttling her around, I tried to create dates. I knew she liked going to clubs, so I worked on my footwork and my flow like I was getting ready for Soul Train. Her twisting and twirling were illegal by most standards, but when I took her dancing, she left the club without me.

Next, I tried to take her to dinner. At the restaurant, she ordered three full entrees. I was kicking myself. This was below my dignity. I was nothing more than gum on her shoes. What was I doing?

On the drive home from Flirty Shirley's dinner (for a small family), we passed through one traffic light after another. As I drove, I thought. Flirty Shirley was in my system like a rare disease. She would surely be my damnation if I continued this way. There had to be a cure for the addiction. Oblivious to my anguish, she was singing and rapping in the front seat.

Up ahead, I saw a churchyard in the distance. I thought, *Perfect! A place to clear my head.* Growing up across the street from Friendship Confederate Cemetery built a boldness within me regarding graveyards. Friendship CC was like a park when we were kids. We played hide-n-seek in there. We raced bicycles. We picked the plums that grew near the river. It was a beautiful and solemn resting place. We meant no disrespect; we were just young and naive with nothing to do. I'm sure my time spent in Friendship added to my darker side.

As I drove through the gates of this new cemetery, Flirty Shirley spun around to the left and to the right. She screeched, "What are you doing?! Why are we here?" I told her I needed a moment. "A moment?! A moment for what?"

I didn't respond, but when I got out, Flirty Shirley quickly hit the door locks. I walked about while she banged on the windows. She flashed the headlights and tooted the horn. I heard her noise but continued to shuffle between the tombs and read the stones. The cemetery calmed me and the weight was lifted. Then, it was time to go.

Flirty Shirley didn't want to let me back into the car. When I turned around to leave on foot, she uncorked a scream that surely rattled the dead. I laughed until I cried. Before long, she relented and let me back into the car.

As I drove off, Flirty Shirley clenched my arm like never before. She was exhausted from fear. She never spoke to me again, but I really didn't care. The dead had broken her spell on me.

Jerry Takes a Bride

Despite his setbacks as a brother, Jerry was quite the ladies' man. As they say, "It was good he was handsome, because he had nothing else to offer." His good looks and magnetic smile got him all the hot chicks. Plus, he wasn't attacked for being the kid of "That Crazy Bicycle Lady" the way Carl, Tommy, and I were. People showered Jerry with gifts, money, and trips beyond anything I could imagine. It was hard not to be jealous.

There were a few of Jerry's type in the neighborhood, and I got to know some of the other pretty boys. They had a fraternal connection to each other, and I had a chance to see the magic up close. My relationships with females were laughable in comparison.

On a trip home from college, Jerry informed me—out of the blue—that he was getting married the following weekend. I was stunned silly. It was such short notice. Then again, nothing Jerry had ever done was logical, so why should things make sense now? I wanted to know: where would the wedding be held? Where would they go on a honeymoon? Where would they reside? And, *who* was he going to marry?

He told me the wedding would be at his bride's house, and they planned to live with her family. I took a deep breath and said I'd try to make it. No promises, but I would do my best.

The next weekend, I got to Columbus the morning of the wedding. I was going to wear my one and only suit that hung in the closet at home. I felt like the cat's meow whenever I put it on, so much so that I actually bought the same suit twice. The first was destroyed by, guess who? That's right, Jerry!

Unbeknownst to me, he snuck out of the house wearing my suit one night, and went to a bar. His drinking had become a problem by that point. Alcohol gave him the liquid courage he otherwise didn't have. He got into a fight at the bar and the suit was ripped beyond repair. Jerry was too irresponsible and entitled to replace it, just like my Torino, so I scraped up enough money to buy the same identical suit a few weeks later.

When I got home for his wedding, I was thunderstruck to find the second suit missing. Jerry had taken my one and only suit, once again without permission. I should have expected as much, but I was so peeved, I boycotted his wedding.

Jerry got married in his stolen suit. He moved in with his bride and her family. I feared what might unfold at his new home because of his abusive drinking and tendency for fighting. He wasn't the type to tone things down just because he was in someone else's house. Unsurprisingly, his first marriage didn't last long.

Campused

I wrecked my Ford Torino in the summer of my sophomore year at MSU. Without a car, I had no means of transportation. I was completely devastated. My classes no longer held my interest and my grades reflected it. I couldn't handle being unable to get around when I needed to.

I stayed on campus more than I wanted because the work-study program was the only way to make money to repair my car. I did everything from being an intramural referee to organizing books at the library. I worked a lot of hours because the pay was meager.

One bonus to being campus bound was a lot of hot co-eds who came in and out of the library. I was depressed, but not blind. There was one girl named Valerie who flirted with me whenever she came in to study or return a book. I was trying my best to be her only friend, but one of my co-workers, Marcus, spent more time with Valerie than I cared for. Marcus was a little shorter than me but he had the physique of a bodybuilder. We conversed occasionally but to me, he was competition.

One Sunday night, after we finished our shift, Marcus invited me out for a joy ride around Starkville. There wasn't much I hadn't seen before but I was bored of my routine. We talked a bit and he delivered the news Valerie already had a boyfriend. I was disappointed and silently curious as to why he wasn't also let down by the news. After all, he spent a lot of time chatting her up at the library. Valerie was cute, charming, sexy, and smart. How come he didn't seem to care?

On our drive, Marcus announced that we were stopping to pick up his roommate, Jackie, who worked at a local hotel. "No problem," I said. Jackie was extremely friendly and quite a talker. I'd seen him around campus, but we'd never met. They invited me up to their dorm room for a beer and a game of cards. I still needed a minute to reset after hearing that Valerie was spoken for, so I said, "Sure, I'll come up for a drink with you guys." Nothing wrong with making new friends.

Back at the dorm, the three of us sat around a makeshift table, playing cards and having a couple of beers.

Out of nowhere, Marcus asked me if I thought Jackie was cute. *What an odd question.* I said, "Jackie seems cool. I'm sure he gets his share of the girls."

Then Jackie asked, "But could you like a guy like me?"

It was an *Oh Crap* moment. I knew then exactly what time it was. Time to get the hell out of there.

I replied, "I think you would be a good friend." I jumped up from the table to beat a retreat, and just then, Jackie started to pull down his pants.

With my voice near shouting, I said, "Dude, Dude, what the hell are you doing? Get your stuff back on!"

I was the furthest person from the door, wedged in the room between a table and a bed. I started overturning objects and tossing chairs to make a path to get out! Jackie was opposite me and tried to cut me off at the exit. He smiled and said, "Just give me a hug." It was poignantly obvious he wouldn't settle for a hug.

I tensed up in combat mode and I told this guy, "You have less than one second to get out of my way." Jackie moved, and I rushed back to my place. I was completely rocked.

How could my fixation on Valerie have turned into a fight or flight moment back in our dorm? I had to get the money together to get my car fixed ASAP and get my ass off campus.

Aiming High

By junior year, I started to unravel like a blown tire on the interstate. Even though I'd gotten the cash together to fix my car, it was never the same. My ride continued to deteriorate, and I didn't have the money to keep up with all the repairs.

I had distanced myself even more from Mom and Aunt Kathy. They were crazier than a pair of roosters in the hen house. My grades fell well below my ability. I always loved school, but I had lost interest. I felt alone, depressed, and for the first time in my life, scared. I desperately needed a shot in the arm.

Like so many other guys in my situation, I decided to join the Air Force. I took the written test and was bussed to Jackson, Mississippi for the physical. The examination was a humiliating process. I had to strip down to nothing to allow a group of doctors to examine my backside. I felt like I'd been publicly molested, but the doctors shook my hand and told me to continue on.

Everything seemed to be moving forward with the physical until I was asked about the burns on my skin. Ultimately, because I'd been scalded as a child due to Mom's negligence, I failed the exam and was denied entry into the U.S. military.

As I rode back to Columbus with the rest of the

applicants, I thought, *What now?* I'd taken my shot and come up mighty short. There were no other cards to play.

I heard a voice in my head say, "It's time to get to know your father." I argued with that voice, because a big part of me wanted nothing to do with him. Another part of me yearned for some direction; from someone, anyone, anywhere. I couldn't go back to school in the state of mind I was in. And so, it was during that ride from Jackson to Starkville, I decided to call my dad. The stage was set.

Let's Talk

I knew where my dad worked – he was a principal at an elementary school – so I called him during business hours. His secretary answered the phone and asked for my name. When I told her, she put me straight through as if she had been expecting my call. When my dad picked up the line, he asked once more who was calling.

It was total recall. I gave him my full name, just like I had when I encountered him at the library. And just like that first run-in, he was stunned silent. Finally, he cleared his throat and told me to meet him at his school the following Saturday. I agreed to be there.

I still hadn't rounded up enough cash to get my car fixed, so I walked the ten miles to his office. I was desperate, broke, and used to walking, so it was no big deal. I was hoping for a good talk and interested to see where things might go. Admittedly, my hopes were off the charts.

My thoughts raced during the long walk to meet him. Life had been a burden; not a joy. I knew I needed therapy in a bad way, but I couldn't go there. I also desperately needed another car. Without one, I had no semblance of a life, no access to bigger and better jobs where I could earn more money.

For some reason, while walking, a sense of relief came over me. I arrived on schedule, wearing my preppie look. My dad and I shook hands and he led me into his office.

The school administrator's office had always been bad juju for yours truly. I flashed back to images of Principal Shell Shock breaking boat paddles and belts on my ass. I struggled to regain my confidence in the face of those memories.

As soon as I sat down, the questions began. This was his turf and his ball game. If I was going to make an impression, I had to walk the tightrope without a pole or a net. He asked what was it that prompted me to call. I told him it was time. Then he went through the same circus as he had previously. He asked about Jerry ("he's fine") and Aunt Kathy ("she's fine too"). In reality, I hadn't spoken with Aunt Kathy since she threatened me with her six-shooter, but I had brought a better poker face to this meeting than I had when I was caught off guard all those years ago.

Because he had his guard up, my dad stood while I sat and watched him pace. I noticed we had the same cow eyes. It was as if I was looking at a reflective time machine. There was no doubt we were related.

We talked for about an hour, but it felt like a week. Finally, he asked, "How can I help you?"

I kept my composure and responded, "Well, I really need a car."

He nodded and said, "Let me see what I can do."

In that moment, I felt so good. I thought maybe he would come through with a car and I could get my life back on track. I wasn't sure how many wishes I would be granted; I needed the work of a gypsy, a soothsayer, and a village shrink to be considered a halfway normal person.

As our meeting came to a close, my dad shook my hand again and said, "You've made my day." I felt a sudden surge of emotion and released a huge smile. Then he added, "Shucks, you've made my whole year!" No one had ever said anything like that to me. No sidekick, girlfriend, or relative.

He offered to drive me home, and we decided to meet again soon. At that point, I was excited. I saw my life taking a new shape. There was hope for a real family, someone to talk to, and maybe even a dollar to line my pockets.

Car Jacked

The following weekend, Dad picked me up at home and brought me to his office. When we got there, he told me he'd spoken with Aunt Kathy. I knew well enough only evil and ignorance came out of that woman.

Immediately, I turned on the poker face. I was twenty-one years old. A man. Why the hell would he talk to that nimrod? Yet, I understood. Aunt Kathy was part of my inner circle and she had known me since I was a baby. It was wise to talk to someone who knew me, but if Aunt Kathy was involved, loose particles of crap would soon follow.

Sure enough, he said, "Aunt Kathy stated if it were entirely up to her, she wouldn't get you a car." I was reaching for my breathing apparatus and almost sank through the floor. I knew she wanted to hurt me, but this was brain surgery with a sling blade. How dare she step on me like that!

I saw Dad was attempting to make a connection between my request and her advice. For me to show anger or disrespect toward Aunt Kathy would have been the kiss of death. I had to just sit there and take it.

Sadly, my nearest and dearest relative had finally gotten even with me for messing with her precious

Jerry. Once again, I was foolish enough to underestimate Aunt Kathy. I was over a barrel. I had to accept defeat and find another way forward.

Dinner at 2:00

I didn't see it coming, but Dad invited me out to his house for dinner, to meet the family. It felt like landing a job after a failed interview.

First, I'd been butchered by Aunt Kathy, "the Christian guardian of the South Side," and the go-to person when it came to me. Of course, her score for me was two thumbs down.

Second, I knew Dad was concerned about my past associations. I was from the Trash Alley. It was my community. I hung out with thugs from the Frog Bottom, the Burns Bottoms, the Red Line, the S-Curve, the Sandfield, the Morning Side, and a bunch of other places that shall remain nameless. I knew all of the "Legends of the Hood": Sin Man, Swap, Boo Boo, Emp-Man, Cookie Man, Shank, Polar Bear, Bae Willy, Bae Bruh, Skullhead Ned, Pimp, Crunch, and Goat Turd (just to name a few). I thought maybe Dad had summoned me as a "show and tell" for the kids in his neighborhood—the hardliner to scare those wayward suburban brats back into reality.

Third, the people in my community never invited anyone for breakfast, lunch, or dinner. I mean never, and especially me. An invitation for a meal was usually part of a grand scheme to embarrass or humiliate me. So, when Dad asked me to come over, I was completely out of my element in every way. I wasn't prepared to meet his family in the slightest.

Regardless, Dad planned to pick me up at 2:00 p.m. on a Sunday afternoon. Surely, I needed a spiritual intervention. That morning before the rendezvous, I headed off to church. I hoped Pastor Keith could work some magic for a troubled wretch like me.

When I entered the church, I was shaking like a dope-man who was in the wrong place with the wrong package. The lead usher that day was none other than my old nemesis, the thug, Teddy Charles. He was standing next to a stained glass window, and his job was to balance the placement of parishioners throughout the church. Teddy Charles guided me toward the front of the church, but I wasn't falling for another one-man crucifixion. I ducked into the first available pew for immediate cover. I hadn't stepped foot into Beacon Central Baptist Church in a long time, and I wanted to slip in as quickly and quietly as possible.

I ended up sitting right next to Sexy Patty. The placement wasn't on purpose. (I needed the hands of God, not a girlfriend.) Since I was dealing with my own issues, I failed to notice that she was clenching a napkin and sweating profusely from head to toe. Nonetheless, she looked hotter than a fever.

The choir stood, and Aunt Kathy led them in her own rendition of Leaning on the Everlasting Arms. The twins, Mary and Martha, sang back up wearing identical hats. These two sisters had put the fear of God in me at a very young age. They had my blessing to sing whatever they wanted to. But it would have taken a pack of Timber wolves to drown out Aunt Kathy.

Sexy Patty looked over and smiled at me. She had a smile that could melt cold butter. Her gaze nearly caused me to request a hymn called I Feel the Fire Burning in my Heart, but I quickly returned focus to my hour of need. I was there for a sign.

Pastor Keith took to the podium and asked the congregation to open their Bibles to Matthew 8:23-27. He preached about Jesus calming the waters on the lake. Again and again, he shouted, "Peace be still! Peace be still!" I felt my nerves coming to a rest.

Out of nowhere, Sexy Patty squeezed my hand with everything she had. I glanced her way only to find out she wasn't hitting on me; she was touched by the Holy Spirit. She threw her hands in the air to wave at Jesus and my hand went up too. Sexy Patty lurched out of her seat to shout and dance, but we were still locked digit to digit. I had no choice but to rise with her. With all her foot stomping, the spikes of her stilettos drove straight through my canvas shoes. I shouted out in pain while hopping on one leg and blurted out, "Jesus, Oh Jesus!" Sexy Patty danced and shouted to the East while I screamed and hopped to the West.

I had planned to go unnoticed in church, but it was too late. Everyone saw the old heathen was back among them. As if that wasn't bad enough, they were so moved by our expressions of the Holy Spirit, a whole section of worshipers got up to hop on one leg too. We had a full Soul Train line bouncing up and down behind us, shouting, "Jesus, Oh Jesus!"

Eventually, Teddy Charles and the other ushers made their way over to us. I knew Teddy Charles relished seeing me in pain. For years, he wanted to get revenge on me for giving him a urine bath. Here I was now, whimpering before him like a hapless child. It was his lucky day.

As I sat there in pain, caressing my foot, I suddenly had a Cinderella moment. The pain brought me back to my senses. Sexy Patty had already inflicted more agony than I could handle.

Meanwhile, all the faithfuls came by to say, "Praise the Lord" and "Just trust in God!" Even Aunt Kathy said, "Bless you, baby." Finally, Pastor Keith stopped by to thank me for stirring the congregation. He stroked my head and said, "God is Good!" I tearfully replied, "All the time."

Church came to a close. I needed to get back home. I didn't want Dad waiting on me. On the way, I ran into Jerry, who was staggering in the opposite direction. I asked him where he was going and he said, "I hear that the church is breaking the wine today."

I told him, "Yes, but Communion is at 6 p.m. You're way too early."

He then asked, "Will they have wine during Commotion?"

"Yes, but it's called Communion. Why don't I walk you home? You can come back later for your blessing."

222

"I don't need the blessing; I just need them to pass me the bottle." He was clearly in a bad way, and I didn't have the heart to tell him he would only get a small sip of wine. I continued home and left him in the street, wondering if Aunt Kathy knew about the terrible state her precious Jerry was in.

After the excitement of the morning and seeing some of the old characters from the neighborhood, it was a relief to get in the car with Dad. As he drove out to his house, everything became a fable. We practically disappeared into the woods. When he opened the door to his home, I stepped onto a cloud. I had never experienced so much tranquility in a house. The silence was deafening.

I almost wanted to make a run for it. Everyone was so nice and cordial, which never happened when I was around. There had to be something sinister at play. I kept looking for an escape hatch, just in case I was in the wrong dimension. I checked the walls for signs of ghosts, devils, dead dogs, and haints. I saw no remnants, nor did I hear any voices. The coast was clear.

The family invited me to stay for a big sleepover. It was a bigger challenge than they could have imagined. I had to bring my own recordings of shooting, stabbing, break-ins, robberies, cussing, fighting, door slamming, cars screeching, and sirens just to get into a sleep mode. After that, I slept like a baby in a manger.

Slowly, that serenity began to soak into my bones. Unbeknownst to everyone, my healing had begun.

Ultimately, Dad did decide to buy me a car. It was a giant step forward, but I always felt as if he was playing defense against me. He was closely guarded, and I found it odd that he never asked about my mom. I wasn't looking for answers, nor did I stupidly want them to get together. I simply wanted an opening to talk to my father about my relationship with my mother. Unfortunately, that door never budged in the slightest.

However, I cherished that first and all the subsequent visits with my dad's family. I sat motionless for hours and tried to rub the peace I found with them all over my face.

The Big Cop Out

I met Amber right before graduating from Mississippi State University. I was still a poor college student. Amber was the love connection I had longed for and we dated for more than a year. She was from a middle-class family and I was a peasant from the wrong side of the tracks. In other words, her parents didn't initially care for this young lover boy.

The first time I went to Amber's suburban home, I was dressed to the nines. I modeled my style from the pages of GQ magazine and thought I looked way better than your typical project kid or local bum. I even walked with an air of confidence. But to her mother, my attire was just lipstick on a pig. She wasn't buying the refurbished me. I felt like she had seen mud on my forehead. Even though I was totally uncomfortable, I held my composure and was respectful. Her mother's attitude was mere water off of this duck's back. I was used to being ostracized.

My dad was a well-respected school principal in Columbus; a lot of families looked up to him. I never talked about him or our growing bond, even to Amber, but out of nowhere, Amber mentioned that I had been seen in the Holly Hills section of the city. She wanted answers as to why I would be on her side of town. I finally gave in and told her I'd been visiting my dad, and told her who he was. The look on Amber's face was to die for. She carried the new information back home to her parents.

The next time I went to Amber's place, I was greeted at the door with a big smile by her mother. This time, I was welcomed and escorted to the "big boy" chair. I was offered drinks and hors d'oeuvres. Since it was Amber's birthday, her dad insisted I take Amber out in his Mercedes and not my Hoop-D. I was shocked stupid. I kept my cool demeanor, but underneath I was saying, "Holy Jesus! What is going on?" I had gone from the outhouse to the penthouse with a mere slip of the tongue.

I took Amber to a fast food joint and respectfully returned her home. We were out and back before her sisters even started their dates. I saw the disappointment on my girl's face, but I had no money. I was still in school and could only promise better things in the future.

I decided to continue my education in the fall of 1982 at Jackson State University. Amber and I continued a long distance relationship well into the summer of 1983. I was in Jackson and she went to a local school. She got into my system like no woman had ever done before. I was determined to make her 'the one'. We were crazy in love. At least that's what I thought.

About a week after a great date in Jackson, a friend told me Amber was engaged to be married. It was poker face time, but I was burning inside. I told the friend, "Oh yes, I knew about her engagement. Amber and I were never meant to be long term." I probably didn't fool him, but I didn't know what else to say.

As soon as my friend was out of sight, I went into overdrive and dug through my pockets for money to call Amber. Just as I found the right change, I thought to myself, *Stop, wait a couple of days, then go to see her. Make it a big pow wow. Something of this magnitude requires a face to face conversation.*

But a funny thing happened on my drive from Jackson to Columbus. I started to measure myself against this new fiancé. He had to have known Amber and her family for some time. The betrayal factor was in full effect. Turned out, the other guy was in the military, which meant he had a steady job, whereas I did not. A soldier has a future that's constantly expanding, whereas my future was still unknown. If I was going to make a last minute play for Amber, I needed more than, "Baby, I love you."

By the time I got to Columbus, I had talked myself into retaining the little dignity I had left. I decided to simply call and congratulate my now ex-girlfriend on her engagement, and be on my way. It was an awkward call, but I did what had to be done. I took the high road instead of holding Amber's feet to the flame.

That was a heartbreak that made me look at myself unequivocally. I was certain that Amber and I were breathing the same air. I would have sworn our hearts beat in rhythm. I would have bet our taste buds were identical. I couldn't wrap my head around what had happened.

About ten years later, I was home for Christmas. I've always had a thing for '70s R&B vinyl records, so I decided to visit the music store. There I was, thumbing through the oldies, when suddenly Amber and I were face to face. We hugged, we cried, and we started to talk about our lives.

After we broke the ice, it was obvious our time had passed, but I still had to know what really happened. I pleaded with her for an explanation. Amber told me she had been deeply in love with me, but she had an unspeakable problem at home. Her father had been molesting most of her girlfriends, and she needed to get as far away from him as possible. So, when an old flame returned to the scene and proposed marriage, she quickly accepted. She said she couldn't afford to squander the opportunity to escape. I wanted to know more, but realized how painful it was for her.

I had found my Amber and gotten due closure. I kissed her goodbye, and climbed into my Mercedes to disappear into the Mississippi Delta.

No Dream Tour

In 1984, I went to meet Jerry and Mom at the state prison in Parchman, Mississippi. My brother, Carl, was doing time there for a murder he committed. Someone from back in our Red Line days had been harassing Carl relentlessly, and my brother had finally reached his limit.

I found out before long that the bully Carl had ended was my old nemesis, Skullhead Ned. Skullhead had been unable to drop his mission for revenge against me, and over the many years in between, he had pushed Carl until the feud ended with Skullhead dead and my brother in prison.

It was a tough situation for me, because I'd faced many tyrants in the neighborhood but never wanted to eliminate anyone. I felt moments of rage at times, but I didn't have it in me to kill my fellow man. I'd protected Carl from so many thugs throughout our childhood, but when I wasn't around, he had taken matters to the extreme.

Parchman was as fortified as any prison in any movie. There were security guards roaming about with high-powered rifles, watching each and every move. As the only maximum-security prison for men in the state, it was no dream tour.

When I got there, Mom had a downcast look on her face. She was undoubtedly spooked. I didn't see Jerry initially, so I searched the parking lot and found him talking to some other visitors. Mom and I were visibly shaken whereas Jerry was tailgating, smoking weed, playing his jams, and getting drunk. He could barely stand. His eyes were watery and bloodshot. I thought, *Why would he come here in such a condition? What will happen when the patrolmen notice? Will they arrest me as well?*

I lost it and screamed at Jerry. "WHY ARE YOU SO DRUNK?"

He just smiled. "Don't worry, my man!"

His words didn't give me an ounce of comfort. I wrestled with the idea of getting in my car and driving back to Jackson. I wouldn't be taken in if I never approached the gate with that idiot. But I decided to stay, only because I knew Mom and Carl needed my support. Dealing with Jerry was more than a handful, but I needed to see my little brother. I had come too far to turn back.

I ushered Jerry in and out of the prison and hoped to God no one noticed his drunken state. We either got lucky or they just didn't care. When we exited the prison, I knew I had to have a heart to heart talk with Jerry. I told him if he spent all of his time being drunk, he would miss out on the important things in life.

"Important things, like what?"

I gave up and headed back to college. If Jerry

didn't watch it, he would end up in Parchman in the cell next to Carl's.

The weirdest thing about that time was I never questioned Carl about what happened or why. I knew I couldn't bring Skullhead Ned back, and I knew I couldn't get Carl out of jail. Even though I didn't pull the trigger, I felt responsible and feckless in the same breath. So why browbeat him over it? Yet, I came to regret not having the conversation.

Carl was murdered within three years of being set free. Even after eliminating the worst bully from our childhood, the demons continued to chase him.

The irony of Carl's short life is that he was the smartest of all of us. Where I had to work hard in school, Carl could miss weeks at a time, then show up and pass any test with flying colors. He was a natural learner with a sharp mind, but our unstable early life cheated him of any foundation to stand on.

Carl's death was the biggest loss I ever suffered. No one knew me like he did. No one could make me laugh like he did. No one challenged me like he had.

I carry my little brother with me each and every day since his departure. I mentally run a lot of my decisions by him. If I'm spotted talking to myself, then I am probably having a family meeting with Carl. His death left me all alone in a cold world.

What Brown Did for Me

When I enrolled in classes at Jackson State University to study Information Systems, it didn't take long to realize I needed an off campus job. My roommate, Larry Battle, was working for UPS. Larry was an ex-football player, which made him well suited for the rigors of package handling. The work was tough, but it paid well and offered good benefits.

UPS actively recruited students for entry-level positions and randomly selected from colleges around Jackson, Mississippi. At the time, JSU was out of the rotation. No one had been interviewed for months, so it was a challenge just to get in front of anyone at the company. Through luck, patience, and his connections, Larry hooked me up with a rare opportunity to work there. Still, I didn't take any chances. So, I drove out to the placement offices at the other schools in the area and put my name on their waiting lists. Within days, I received a call, passed the interview, and went to work.

I should have known the job would be rigorous for the money they were shelling out. On the first night, I was instructed to unload boxes from the bed of an eighteen-wheeler at a rate of thirteen hundred packages per hour, with temperatures north of one hundred degrees. Being new to the job, it didn't take long for me to dehydrate and fizzle out. I'd never worked so hard in such a short interval in my life. I only lasted about an hour and twenty minutes that first night. The shift was four hours without a break. I cheated the company out of two hours and forty minutes.

I stumbled out of the warehouse toward my car, aching in places I didn't know I had. Larry had too much fun watching me fall on my face. I was so fatigued, I sat on the ground against my car for thirty minutes before trying to drive off the lot. Once I got home, I called my girlfriend and asked her to walk on my back until I fell asleep. If I was going to keep that job, I needed to up my game.

Someone forgot to tell Larry and UPS there was NO QUIT in me! Two months later, I was one of the top unloaders on the crew, even though I was the smallest. A year later, UPS encouraged me to join the management team, but I was still in college with other ideas. I'd met a recruiter named John Burkett from the Federal Aviation Administration (FAA), and he persuaded me to try a career in Air Traffic Control. This was a civil service position where I would get paid well, have more security, and garner the respect of those who doubted me. I was determined to get an apprenticeship and test it out.

Meanwhile, I made good use of the benefits at UPS. The company insurance paid the initial fee for braces on my teeth; badly needed after eating junk food most of my life. I got surgery for the burn scars that covered 30% of my body. The company even held a slot for me when I took the apprenticeship with the FAA. I gave my all just to get on board with UPS and it returned with life-altering dividends.

Even then, my career in Air Traffic Control was calling.

PART VII:
MEMPHIS BLUES

The Search

Dylan sat, mesmerized. I have to say, for all my doubts when he first approached me, he turned out to be a good listener. Recalling the details of my past, though painful, was cathartic.

When I stopped for breath, Dylan signaled to the beachside barman for another round. Surely, we had drained the entire liquor stash by now. I don't know where he put it all. Hell, I don't know where I put it all either.

When two fresh margaritas arrived, Dylan said, "Now, my friend, I think we're getting somewhere. I've been dying to know what hell you must have endured that would propel you to voluntarily walk into a war zone. At the risk of sounding obvious, do you think it's because you were fleeing from your own war at home?"

I had long passed the point where his calling me "friend" was irritating. By now, it was a comfort. No one else had ever sat and listened to my crazy stories, one after the other, with such attention.

In response to his inquiry, I said, "Dude, there aren't enough therapists in the world to answer that question. Maybe. It's possible. That idea has been floated by others before."

We both looked out at the inky water. The afternoon had faded to early evening and darkness was settling in. Most of the other beachgoers had left for the day. It was just us and the seagulls now and a sailboat on the horizon. A chill went through me.

I said, "Hey man, should we pack it in? These stories will keep. I've carried them with me long enough. Another day won't change anything."

"What, are you crazy? We just got new drinks! I'll wrap myself in my beach towel and stay out here all night."

"If you say so, brother."

"Tell me. Did you and your buddies ever find those missing coworkers after the blast?"

"Ahh, yes. Back to that. Sorry, I keep getting waylaid in the telling of that story. Let's see if we can't put a bow on it this time."

And so, I went back again to the cold, dark streets of Afghanistan...

Before I left with the search party, I grabbed a jacket and a flashlight from my room. It was freezing and pitch black outside. Without the torch, our rescue efforts would have been futile. The whole city had lost electricity and only the emergency generators hummed and whirred inside the Safe Room. It was like walking through a landfill or a junkyard at night after someone smashed out the security lights. Every step required extreme caution. We all knew the perimeter well, but on that night, it was utterly foreign.

Word spread that two more of our coworkers were missing. That made four people unaccounted for. Apparently, Dale was barricaded in her room. Charlotte and Mack were reportedly trapped at the bar, and Derrick was last seen near the gym.

We went for Dale first. When we got to her room, we heard moans. She was calling for help with the little energy she had left. We tried to kick her door open but it didn't budge. Luckily, her room was on the first floor so we climbed in through the window. She was lying on the floor, covered with debris. She was trapped under a table and a dresser, dust, glass, and a shattered 40-inch TV. She indicated that she suffered from severe back pain. It wasn't wise to move her. So, we cleared away as much debris as possible. Then we made a passage to the door.

The nurse wanted to take Dale to the military hospital, but the roads were impassable. We'd have to carry her on foot, and the hospital was three miles away. Our camp wasn't safe, but the territory outside the zone was far more risky. Yet, Dale needed immediate medical attention. We enlisted four volunteers to take Dale to the entrance of the military base on a stretcher. They made it to the gate and back safely.

Next, we went after Charlotte and Mack at the bar. Miraculously, Charlotte had only sustained cuts and scrapes. We found her standing where the bar had once been. She looked as if she was waiting for a taxi, but she was so badly shaken, she hardly said a word. Later, Charlotte recounted she had been serving a drink to Mack when suddenly, she found herself standing alone outside. The rest of the building had been obliterated in the blast.

We tried to find out if Charlotte knew Mack's whereabouts. She thought he was somewhere in the bar, but she hadn't seen him since the explosion. We called out his name and he called back faintly in return—a good sign. We pushed through the rubble to find Mack on a stool where our watering hole used to be. He was just sitting there, distraught, waiting for his third Jack and Coke.

Mack said, "I lost my glasses." We kept him talking so he would remain calm. He told us, "I was sitting at the bar with Charlotte when suddenly the floor disappeared. I hurt my back while climbing onto my seat. In the process, I emptied my last shot!"

Our nurse wanted Mack moved to the military hospital as well. Unlike Dale, Mack was six feet, two inches tall and two hundred and forty pounds – a tall order by any standards. Luckily for Mack, the same gurney crew agreed to take him.

The only thing holding me up during the search effort was adrenaline. Without it, I would have been too exhausted to continue. I'd been involved in many hustles and work details in my time, but none as death defying as that night.

During the rescue operation, I thought back over the challenges I'd faced in my early career, my struggle to find lasting love, and the never-ending family drama that had followed me from childhood into adulthood. My mind was swimming in those memories as our search continued through the night.

The Big Interview

After being selected for an apprenticeship with the FAA, I was invited for an official interview at Jackson International Airport. I didn't have a business suit, but I put together a nice ensemble that was sure to pass. I got to the place on time and sat down with the chief of Medgar Evers Field. He showed me the layout of the FAA Air Traffic Control system and informed me I had not yet been assigned to an official work facility. The information was welcome as far as I was concerned. I just wanted a job; I had no idea what Air Traffic Controllers actually did. I figured I would learn as I went and make adjustments as necessary.

Next, the chief told me about the work environment. He said most of the employees had very little tact and even less prior interaction with minorities. My gleaming eyes dimmed. I sensed something problematic at hand.

The chief went on to give me an example of what he called "cultural ignorance". He admitted he had been at a Christmas party with a few African Americans and requested "more nigger toes". He stared at me for a reaction and I stared back at him, trying to decode the term. I held my poker face but I'd never heard the expression before. After a moment of silence, I conceded ignorance. He said the term was used for Brazil nuts and confessed it was the only racial slur he'd ever used.

I just shook my head. Obviously, I was in a whole new arena.

The chief went on, "I have another example for you."

I sat up and cleared my throat. "Ok, go ahead."

"A lot of these guys (he meant white guys) from the FAA are down home Southerners. If you come and work here, you'll hear the term 'coon-ass' a lot." He explained they toss that insult around daily without thinking, and insisted they didn't use it to be racial.

Horrified, I locked eyes with him again, and tried to regain that poker face of mine. I gathered myself and repeated, "Coon-Ass, huh?" He nodded affirmatively and said the term was used to describe a "backward redneck" – another expression I'd never heard.

The chief had one last humdinger to lay on me. "You may hear FNG quite a bit."

I was perplexed. "What's that?"

Without hesitation, "Freaking Nigger."

I nearly fell out of my seat and I'm sure my heart skipped a beat, but I maintained composure. I kept wondering to myself, *What year is it? Are people really still like that? Do I want to venture into this?*

As much as my head was spinning, I wanted this job very badly. I decided right then and there, *Such is the world I live in, so I better toughen up.*

I knew the chief wanted some kind of reaction from me. I reached within and said, "Sir, I've been around white people all my life. Yes, I've hit some rough patches from time to time and I've heard my fair share of slurs, but I can cope with anyone and anything."

The chief smiled. "Well, if that's the case, welcome to the FAA!"

When I left the interview, instead of elated that I'd just landed the job I'd been coveting for quite some time, I felt completely drained by the things I'd just learned. I wasn't into church or liquor, but I needed a prayer and a drink if I was going to accept the position. My demeanor must have impressed the chief, though. Shortly thereafter, I was assigned to the Memphis Air Route Traffic Control Center. It wasn't as Deep South as Mississippi where I'd grown up, but what I encountered in Memphis was more shocking than anything I'd endured down there.

Memphis Center

I don't think anything can fully prepare you for pure, raw racial prejudice. I'd faced intimidation many times before, but racism is a special kind of bullying. If you happen to have a dark complexion in a sea of white people, there's nowhere to hide. It's like a deer trying to play opossum with a wolf. When you're on the menu, the trick won't work.

It didn't matter how professional or cordial I was to my co-workers, I was not welcome at Memphis Center. From the get-go, I was either on edge or trying to decipher someone's intentions. To say I was jumpy is an understatement.

I started out dispersing flight plans (information about the airplanes' destination) to different work sectors. Between deliveries, someone asked if I liked the job better than I liked picking cotton. Being that I'd never picked cotton before, I had no point of comparison. But the message was clear. I had no real choice but to go with it. So I said, "Of course." If I was going to make it, then I had to pick my battles, and ignorant racial slurs was not going to be one of them.

A lot of other things went on that posed more of a challenge than in any other place I'd worked before. There were specific customs and quirks that I had to observe and learn.

Every morning, I brought a copy of *The Commercial Appeal* and *USA Today* to work. I was a conscientious and daily newspaper reader. One morning, I placed my papers on the table in the break room and went to get my breakfast. When I returned, most of my favorite sections of the papers were gone. I thought, "What the hell?" I came to find out that the controllers freely took sections from a paper no one appeared to be reading. It was a tradition I learned right there on the job. I also learned to take my papers with me until I had finished reading them.

To be an Air Traffic Controller, you have to have aptitude, vision, courage, and confidence running through your veins around the clock. Most controllers are Type A personalities with the arrogance of fighter pilots. As a minority, I had to be polite and political just to get a shot. Also, air traffic controlling is not a job easily mastered without military experience. I was the net zero apprentice in that regard.

My crew supervisor didn't call me by name for two years. He told my trainers, "Take him to that sector," or "You train that guy," or "How's that fella doing?" I really didn't care if he talked to me or not. I didn't care if he used my name. I only wanted the job. Above all, I wanted a fair chance to prove myself.

One night, I had what I thought was a small run-in with a group of controllers on the midnight shift. They were using racial epithets I found highly offensive. I asked the supervisor-on-duty to have them move their conversations to another area away from my ears.

By sunrise they had turned the story on me. They accused me of being a militant and calling them racists. Most bullies are not that cunning, but these guys were. I left work in a disgusted mood that stayed with me for hours.

It's not like I hadn't dealt with bullies before. I faced them almost every day growing up in Mississippi. Bullies are intimidating and territorial. I was an outsider. If I was going to break in, I had to beat them at their own game. Bullies also ignore you, but I needed them to engage with me if I was going to learn their craft.

I thought I'd drive to Houston, Texas for the weekend, to hang out with my college roommate and cool my jets. After traveling for six hours, I stopped to refuel at a gas station in Denham Springs, Louisiana. At the pump, I heard someone shout, "Boy, you need to hang up the pump!" I couldn't believe what I was hearing. The situation at work combined with that "Boy" statement put me at my tipping point. It was just too insulting. Someone was going to get an ass-kicking.

I marched into the convenience store with anger and determination. I kicked the door open and yelled, "I don't know who the hell y'all think you're screwing with." There were about seven customers in line. All eyes were on the raving lunatic standing in the doorway. A very small white lady at the counter spoke up with a squeaky voice and said, "I was just trying to get this young man to tell my son, Leroy, to hang up the gas pump." I wanted to hide behind the magazine rack out of embarrassment. I apologized for the disturbance and left the store. I was too embarrassed to even buy gas. I drove to another station down the street and continued on to Houston.

On the drive back to Memphis a few days later, I devised a plan that would give me a better than average chance of breaking in with the fraternity of controllers. First, I would make sure I was on point with my knowledge of Air Traffic Control. If I knew my stuff in the field, they were less likely to mess with me. Second, I would learn something about their hobbies so I could hold conversations beyond work. They all had interests like carpentry, mechanics, or lawn care. When appropriate, I would bowl them over with my sharp wit and sense of humor. And as a third measure, I would carry my Bible around at work. These guys had the fear of God in them, no matter how tough they appeared on the outside.

I'm not sure how effective my schemes to fit in were, but somehow, I made it through each day. The other controllers were still distant and even combative at times, but I had climbed a mountain at Memphis Center.

Although it was most definitely a toxic environment, I was in the top 10% income earners in the United States. Up until then, I'd lived my whole life watching others like a prisoner behind "Walls" my mom yelled and barked at. I had broken free from the bondage of being poor; of being bullied and pushed aside; of wearing hand-me-downs and eating off food stamps. As an air traffic controller, for the very first time, I felt like my own man, in control of my life.

Tapping Out

When I got to Memphis in the fall of 1986, I left the dream life of college behind. There were no more beautiful co-eds floating around. I was in the real world now, and being a young professional in a blue-collar city wasn't a good mix for me. I was lonely and miserable. It wasn't a good time for me or my social life. Even though I was earning money and I'd learned how to manage the bullies at work, I never really fit in or made friends there. It was a never-ending struggle to prove myself.

Even the women I dated made me feel empty and depressed. Adela was a prime example. I met her through a co-worker (and to this day, I question that co-worker's intent). To be sure, she wasn't the sharpest knife in the drawer, but she was sexy and a step up from some of the girls I'd previously dated. When I met her, I figured, *why not?*

Once I got to know Adela, I learned she was a religious zealot. Her friends and family were of the same mindset. They always tried to 'out-Christian' one another. If one person said, "Praise the Lord" then the other had to top it with, "Praise the Lord and Thank you, Jesus!" Or someone would say, "Oh, help me Lord," then a voice would say, "Help me Lord. You are an angel of mercy on high." Or, someone would say, "Jesus carried me today," and suddenly someone would jump up doing the church dance while screaming, "Won't he do it, Lord! Won't he do it!"

If you were not from their faith, then you were never good enough or Christian enough to be accepted. It didn't matter who you were or what you did. If you didn't espouse their beliefs then you were on the Highway to Hell. Adela was a constant crusader. Given the chance, she would spread her gospel non-stop to each and every ear about the sins of mankind.

Attending church was Adela's idea of a dream date. I accepted her invitation because I wanted to impress her, plus I wanted to see it all for myself. I was dressed and ready to go hours before the service. There wasn't a chance in hell I was going to miss being in that sanctuary. Similar to Beacon Central Baptist Church, people were dancing, stomping, and shouting up and down the aisles, but Adela's church was praise and devotion on steroids.

Adela was restless because she wanted to join in. She was worried about my perception of her, so I kept my focus on the choir and the pastor as a way to ease her tension. I even tried to sing along with the church hymns, but all the songs were foreign to me. It was useless trying to fake it. There were highs and lows in every verse that made me a dead giveaway.

One of the church members, Sister Baba, roared like a truck engine whenever she felt the Holy Spirit. Everyone watched in anticipation. They would ratchet up the celebrations with the intent of getting Sister

Baba to her tipping point. It didn't take a whole lot. Sister Baba gave back as much as the audience put into it. She loudly started her engine, stepped in gear, and roared like a convoy of big rigs. She drowned out the rest of the congregation all by herself.

Without my approval, Adela volunteered me as the church tambourine player. I had no interest in the job. I was even more dismayed that Adela threw my name in the hat without asking me. Things got tricky after that.

At Thanksgiving, Adela asked me to drive her to her parents' home in Indianola, Mississippi. I should have known something was awfully strange when I picked her up. She had a distant and silent aura about her. Still, I greeted her with, "Hello, pretty lady." She only gave me a wave hello in return; no words came out of her mouth. I tried several different openings but she said very little. I didn't know if she was trying to ration her words or if she'd met her quota for the day.

Because I'd gained no points on our church date, I decided to make another play to win Adela over. This time I would show off my knowledge of famous people and popular places along our route. I started out by showing her Graceland, the home of Elvis Presley, on our way out of Memphis, but Adela had no interest in the King of Rock and Roll. Even when I mentioned that he'd once had a number one selling gospel album, she casually shrugged her shoulders.

When we entered Mississippi, I showed her where Jerry Lee Lewis lived. That landmark made little impression. I couldn't believe she'd never heard the song, *Great Balls of Fire*, so I gave her my personal version of the hit. She just stared at me as if I was having a conniption.

I had no choice but to get on Highway 64 and push onward toward her home. As we traveled through Clarkdale, I told her Morgan Freeman had an estate there. That fell on deaf ears, too.

After about three hours, we passed through Itta Bena, Mississippi, the birthplace of B.B. King. Adela had no love for the Master of the Blues! She hardly said a word the entire trip and didn't share any information about her family. Adela was one tough nut to crack.

As we got to her parents' driveway, I was on edge. The lack of conversation and my obvious failure to impress her didn't bode well. I didn't know what to expect, but I knew my time with her family would be brief.

When the car came to a stop, Adela bolted out of the car to greet and hug her relatives. I was left alone to drag all of her luggage to the door. What I didn't see was her severely mentally challenged brother approaching me like a pitbull. As I opened the trunk and started gathering Adela's things, I was suddenly attacked from behind. Her brother put me in a sleeper hold, and he was as strong as an ox. I was twisting and foaming at the mouth while this guy was yelling like Tarzan of the Apes.

I'd been in a lot of fights before and I knew how to break a chokehold, but it required putting a serious hurt on the guy. I decided to take one for the team. I knew if I put him down then my first impression would be a hostile one, so I hung on until Adela's family finally subdued him.

It was fair to say that I was tapped out on Adela and her bizarre behavior. I left her in the driveway and drove back to Memphis for yet another thankless Thanksgiving.

Ossie May

Another loco chick in my dating repertoire was Ossie May. I met her on the way to work one morning when she forced me off the road with her vehicle. Once out of the car, she cornered me and asked for my name and number. That should have been a clue of what I was in for, but I was lonely and still new to Memphis.

There was nothing ordinary about Ossie May. She was tall, sexy, smart, and pretty. Her looks and personality were her drawing cards. The flip side was her temperament. She was beauty and rage sandwiched together, and she must have invented cussing. She would unload swear word after swear word in rapid succession. There had to be a law against such offensive language.

On our first date, she went into a full-scale meltdown. I don't even remember what it was about, but I took her home and vowed never to see that crazy woman again. My pledge had just one major flaw—she knew where I lived. She showed up the next day. And the next. And the day after that. She knew my friends and my co-workers. There was no getting rid of her.

Ossie May was pure bad news. She showed up repeatedly, uninvited and unannounced. She was everywhere and nowhere I wanted her to be. I had no choice but to see her. She was my bully and my stalker.

One other thing—she was always armed. Ossie May talked about her gun even more than she bragged about her cooking. Out of nowhere, she took me to the gun range. She finished one clip with her right hand then unloaded the other clip with her left. I certainly got the message. She was not to be messed with or messed over. I was scared straight by this woman.

Ossie May infiltrated my life in every way. She made my schedule. She picked my friends. She enforced a curfew! She was preparing me for an O-M tattoo when I was suddenly rear-ended by an uninsured motorist. I battled whiplash for six months. During my recovery time, I rediscovered myself and had to give Ossie May the slip, but no one had ever left Ossie May and survived. At least no one on record. Still, it had to be done.

The problem was, I had no experience dumping anyone. I was always the dumpee, not the dumper. The closest I'd come to a breakup was when I spooked Flirty Shirley at the cemetery. It worked the first time, so why not give it another go?

I waited for the right time. It came at 3:00 a.m. when she called from work and demanded I drive her home. I said, "Sure, I'm on my way." Ossie May started in on her insults and threats as I drove down Horn Lake Road. She compared me to animals and idiots. She said words I dare not repeat; terms that Britannica, Webster's, and Wikipedia don't allow.

She was mid-sentence when she realized we'd just driven past a tombstone. I guided the car into a local cemetery knowing full well how much she hated them. She clutched my hand as the car came to a rest between the crypts. She was as stiff as a board. I was in my element now. I suggested we get out and take a look around.

"Like Hell!" she yelled.

I felt more and more empowered by the minute and decided to have some fun. I told her I wanted to step out and gather some flowers for her. She screamed, "I don't need or want any damn flowers!"

Out of fear, she machine gunned a battery of swear words I'm sure violate every cursing manual. Her profane assault came so fast and strong, I literally ducked and dodged as she spewed out her garbage. Up until that point, she had never attempted to physically harm me, but I felt bruised and battered anyway.

I had to get out. When I reached for my door, she collared my throat, pulled her gun, and took the keys. I grabbed her weapon, redirected it onto her, and dared her to breathe. Ossie May's cussing turned to tears and whimpers. She begged and begged me to leave the cemetery.

I held strong and took my moment. I said, "Ossie May, I will only leave this cemetery when you promise to disappear from my life forever. No more showing up at my house. No more showing up at my work. This is it. You've crossed the line for the last time.

Now, let me hear you promise or you can spend the night here with the devil for all I care."

Stunned and furious that she'd been beaten in her own bullying game, Ossie May nodded and said, "I promise. I'll disappear. This is the last you'll see of me."

And with that I drove her home, removed the bullets from her gun, and handed it back to her. Those dead dogs, devils, and haints that had haunted my mother for so many years had finally stepped in to help a brother out.

Moving On

Three years after I started my career with the FAA, and after the disastrous dating experiences I had in Memphis, I met my kids' mother. We had our first child out of wedlock in 1989. I was not ready to be a husband or a parent. I was completely distracted by stresses of the job and the work environment at Memphis Center, which kept me on edge. People got fired daily, and I didn't want to blow the opportunity after all I'd done to make it work.

After my daughter was born, my dad made it clear he disapproved of my life choices. My irresponsibility in becoming a parent was the only vision he had of me. I was disappointed by his assessment and even more disappointed by how he viewed my daughter. I was a grown man and could handle whatever he thought of me, but no one was going to treat my little princess as less than.

Our relationship unraveled at warp speed. I decided to write him a letter, laying out our troubled history. I wasn't accustomed to needing or seeking approval from him and I wasn't going to start now. In my letter, I told him I was stepping away from his world and I apologized for the intrusion.

I took the letter to a secretarial service. They typed the letter without correcting any of my grammatical or spelling errors. I stood in the store trying to proofread the pages while tears of frustration began to well. The office came to a standstill as they watched me have a full meltdown.

The letter was long and hard to read, but I had poured my entire truth into it. Re-reading it made me emotional. I dashed into the restroom to gather myself and tried to protect the pages from further smears. It was a tough letter to send, but it was time to move on.

I'd spent most of my life feeling conflicted about my father. In some ways, I wanted to be just like him because he was good looking, funny, and successful. He had a secure job and money in the bank. He didn't know anything about the world of poverty he'd left me to be raised in. Getting to know him and his family when I was in college had given me tremendous peace.

When my daughter was born, I realized I was like Dad in ways I didn't want to be. He, too had a child out of wedlock. I guess his own experience was why he was so down on me when I did the same thing. He knew what the scenario looked like; he'd been there. The realization of these similarities snapped me into decision mode. I was determined to be there for my kid, which meant I had to be there for her mom as well.

Suddenly, the ball was in motion. I would win back my baby's mama and make her my wife. It didn't matter if I loved her or not. My focus was on my daughter, not my bride. It was insane, really, but I didn't care. There was no way my daughter was going to grow up without a father the way I had. I was taking the reins.

Of course, it was only a matter of time before trouble reared its ugly head.

Jerry Remarries

Sometime around 1990, I received word that Jerry had remarried. I hadn't seen him for some time, so I had to track him down and find out where he was living. So, I called ahead to let Jerry know I was in town and will be stopping by to see him.

When I got to his duplex, the woman who opened the door was someone who can best be described as the sidekick of Big Foot. She was a beast like none I had ever laid eyes on before. I was polite but cautious as I proceeded to the back room where Jerry was sitting. The years of hard drinking had taken quite a toll. He didn't even resemble the handsome man he once was.

Jerry asked if I'd met his wife, Barbara, at the door, and I nearly pissed my pants. There was nothing attractive about that lady. She wasn't a looker, nor shapely, nor personable. How in the hell had this happened? How had he wound up with such a monster? What was the ransom? This was the guy with strapping good looks who had an unlimited stream of cute and sexy women in his teen years. Mind you, if you stripped Jerry of his looks, the woman who opened the door would be par for the course. But she was not the norm I had come to expect.

Unlike Jerry's first wife and marriage, Barbara was the spouse abuser this time. My nephew told me circumstances where Jerry was the one who had to seek shelter due to Barbara's rages. I believed his stories. Barbara looked able to whip asses well outside of her weight class. I never dared to cross her. I'm sure I would have been a small tassel in her trophy case of destruction. This lady was more suited for challenges of the Big Game variety. Yet Jerry allowed liquor and stupidity to rattle Barbara's cage when others would have fled.

Where's Barbara?

Two months later, I received a desperate call from Aunt Kathy. Jerry was gravely ill. She said Jerry and his wife had been fighting and she feared Barbara had poisoned him. Naturally, I feared for his wellbeing. But logically, why would Barber need to poison Jerry when she could just as easy beaten his ass beyond recognition.

Of course, no one cared for Jerry's best interests like Aunt Kathy. According to her, someone was always doing something to Jerry. Nothing was ever his fault.

Aunt Kathy said Jerry was fading fast, and I should come right away. I'd been taken in by her assumptions before, but felt I shouldn't take any chances. He was my brother. I had already lost Carl, when he was stabbed over a money dispute. His death was such a loss, it had led me to distance myself from the whole family. Now that Jerry was in trouble, I thought it would be wise to do what I could to help him.

I asked Aunt Kathy who was looking after Jerry's four little girls. She said, "Barbara will take care of the twins." I didn't dare remind her that Jerry and Barbara actually had four daughters, but the other two had already learned to fend for themselves.

I told my wife what was going on, took time off from work, and drove the one hundred and sixty miles from Memphis to Columbus, Mississippi to pick up my brother. Aunt Kathy instructed me to take Jerry to the VA Hospital in Jackson. This scene was all too familiar. I'd been with Jerry at the same hospital in the fall of 1985. Now it was 1997.

Back then – just before classes started at Jackson State University – Jerry had come home drunk one night and started a fight with Carl. I tried to stay out of it until Jerry grabbed a mayonnaise jar and threw it at Carl. As I rushed at Jerry, he ran out of the apartment and fell over the railing, landing one floor below. He was unconscious with sandwich spread smeared all over his hands and face. I got him in the car and rushed him to the local hospital in Columbus. I left him in the doctor's hands and headed back to school. I drove the one hundred and fifty miles to Jackson in the dead of night.

A day later, I was informed that Jerry had been sent to the VA Hospital due to swelling on the brain. Destruction was following me! I rushed back to see Jerry right away. When I got to the hospital, he was sitting straight up in bed, staring forward in a daze. He looked completely lost in the head. He was slurring all of his words. He didn't even recognize me. Despite his outward signs, the doctors said that Jerry had improved dramatically and assured me he would make a speedy recovery.

Now, twelve years later, I was heading back to a familiar place. When I got to Columbus, Jerry was awfully weak. He spent most of the drive to Jackson in and out of sleep. At the VA Hospital, I was told they were not seeing any more patients, so I pleaded with one of the doctors and through God's grace, this physician relented and took Jerry in.

About an hour later, it was determined that Jerry had the flu. I was relieved but furious. I had been pulled out of work and taken away from my own family when all he needed was some medicine and rest. With this diagnosis, Jerry got stronger by the hour and was released.

On the drive back to Columbus, he started to talk about his life with Barbara. He said she probably wouldn't even be home when we got back because on Saturdays, she went to the club. It was hard to tell if he was angry Barbara wasn't staying at home with their kids, or mad about being left out. I couldn't tell which.

We arrived at his house around 7 p.m., and just as he had predicted, Barbara wasn't there. All four children (ages three through nine) were home alone. I told Jerry not to worry and to focus on the kids. Between his drinking and Barbara's erratic and violent outbursts toward him, those poor children had no stability. It was all too familiar. Even after being raised and groomed by Aunt Kathy-The Better Parent- Jerry was no more responsible than our mom had been.

Without a clue of what to say to add comfort, I said, "Jerry, if you hear of any Big Foot sightings, you'll know where to look for your wife."

With that, I got in my car and headed back to

Memphis. It didn't take the great Jerry long to release Barbara and find a new bride with four additional kids. I was torn between congratulating him, feeling sorry for his kids, or fearing for the livelihood of the new Mrs. Jerry.

Doing Hard Time

Things weren't necessarily much better back at home. In 1998, my wife and I got into a spat over her misuse of money. She had the notion if she walked away from an argument, the problem would go away as well. She thought if there was no one there to fuss with, I would eventually calm myself down and get over it. Well, not this time. This time, I demanded an explanation about her spending habits. She kept trying to avoid me, but I grabbed her arm to make her face me. She jerked away and retreated to another room in the house.

I gave up and went to watch college basketball in the bedroom. It was Friday evening, so I unwound down to my T-shirt and boxers.

Unbeknownst to me, my wife had instructed our daughter to dial 911 if I ever laid a finger on her. It was the darndest thing, since I had never once touched my wife in anger. Yet, it all happen on cue. Within no time, the doorbell rang. It was the Memphis Police Department. They came in and asked questions about domestic violence. It was only a few years after O.J. Simpson put the stamp on spousal battery. If the cops were called, someone had to be removed from the home.

The Memphis PD saw a smear where I had grabbed

my wife's arm and, just like that, I was handcuffed in my T-shirt and boxers. I pled with the officers for some clothes. They finally relented and let me grab a shirt and a pair of trousers. I wasn't about to be hauled down to the station wearing next to nothing.

Even for a man who had been humiliated by Mom for so many years, I was embarrassed. I was taken downtown and booked on simple assault charges. It had been thirty-four years since my first time behind bars. This time, I had more cellmates than just my mom. When I was four years old, my mom and I were arrested for trespassing onto a dumpsite. Mom was scurrying through the trash for things of value while the workers tried to clear the lot. Since Mom wouldn't heed their commands, the cops were called and we were taken to the Columbus jail. Since there wasn't a shelter for kids in the city, I was tossed in the slammer too.

Here I was, a grown man, placed in a cell with twenty-two other people and one open toilet. Out of sheer luck or God's grace, I didn't have to use the restroom for two days. Unfortunately, I wasn't going anywhere yet.

I didn't speak to anyone, but had to assume I was among real criminals. I immediately put on my poker face and did my best to avoid any eye contact. We were served tuna or peanut butter sandwiches for breakfast, lunch, and dinner. I wanted nothing to do with that place, especially the food. One of my cellmates noticed I wasn't eating and requested I give him my sandwiches. I didn't promise him anything; I just shrugged my shoulders in a maybe.

The guards paced to and fro while cellmates yelled to make phone calls or complain of injuries. Sometimes, they just yelled for attention.

Saturday morning arrived and I hadn't slept a wink. The number of people in the cell was unhealthy for all involved, so the guards let us out into the hallway, to stretch for about two hours. During that time, we all tried to place unauthorized calls to relatives or friends.

I happened to be next in line for the phone when a big female guard told us to step away. I tried to plead my case, being next and all, but the big guard stated, "If anyone says another damn word, they'll be back in their cell."

I was too close to give up, so I blurted out, "Ma'am, Ms. Ma'am! Can I please just make one call?" She screamed back, "Get your damn ass in that damn cell!" I thought, *Wow, this is crazy* but then I realized I was in the cell all by myself. I could finally get some sleep in peace.

Later that night, for reasons I didn't understand, I was taken upstairs and put in a cell alone. As the time ticked by, I buried my head in the pillow and asked myself, "How in God's name did this happen?"

When I was finally released on Sunday morning, my wife was there to pick me up. I said very little. I couldn't wait to shower, shave, and eat something for the first time since Friday.

At the hearing, my lawyer got my case expunged with the agreement I would go to Anger Management classes. I thanked my attorney with a smile and thought, anything to stay out of the slammer. That was no place for me.

Even the Devil Needs a Heart

S hortly after my stint in jail, Aunt Kathy needed a quintuple bypass operation. Until then, I had never heard of more than a quadruple heart surgery. She was somewhere around seventy-three years old and I didn't have much confidence she would survive the operation.

True to character, Aunt Kathy had an iron clad air of determination. She wouldn't even entertain a conversation about "What if?"

Surprisingly, when I was alone, I did shed some tears. Aunt Kathy was the only real family I had known and the only person Mom cared about at all. I knew she didn't care for Mom with the same enthusiasm, but now was not the time to focus on her shortcomings. I told myself I should bury the hatchet and be the best nephew I could be under the circumstances, which is exactly what I did. I was very attentive during her recovery, staying with her morning and night. I prayed with her at dust and dawn.

She asked me to call the people she considered close to her: Uncle Dan, Jerry (duh), Pastor Keith, and a fellow church member. Uncle Dan was Mom and Aunt Kathy's youngest sibling. He and Aunt Kathy were like Satan and Damien. Her influence over Uncle Dan even extended to his own kids. His wife took ill when their six girls were little and she never returned home to take care of them. Uncle Dan was their sole caregiver for the rest of their childhood, but he only showed his youngest daughter any love. In fact, he drove a wedge between them all, so they didn't even have each other to rely on. Aunt Kathy mirrored his lack of affection for the kids, and I'm convinced she encouraged their division.

The brother and sister duo were so deeply connected, they even went so far as to sign their properties over to each other. Their shared mission was to prevent Dan's children or anyone in my family from having claims on their stuff. Their greed and conniving knew no limits. Given their bond, Uncle Dan was my first call. When he answered the phone, I got the impression I was interrupting something. He was eerily silent when he heard the news about Aunt Kathy's impending and dangerous operation. It struck me as odd that he didn't ask a single question or request to stay informed.

Next, I called Pastor Keith, whom Aunt Kathy loved as much as God himself. He had been the minister of our church since 1965. When I called to tell him about Aunt Kathy's condition, he was so quiet I wondered if he was still on the phone. There was no, "Praise the Lord" or "Trust in God!" There was no, "me and my flock will be calling on high for her recovery." For the first time since I had known him, Pastor Keith was without words. And just like Uncle Dan, he didn't ask any questions, extend any well wishes, or request I keep him updated. He never inquired what hospital she was in or what room number—nothing.

Admittedly, I was totally startled by Uncle Dan and Pastor Keith's reactions, or lack of reactions as it turned out. I called the church member and her reception was one of concern and prayer. My last call was my brother, Jerry. He listened, but also said nothing. I shared my unprofessional prognosis for Aunt Kathy and my concern, but still, he gave no response.

The night before the operation, I called everyone once again. I thought this was their final chance to say something before Aunt Kathy passed away. Uncle Dan and Pastor Keith remained unfazed. Jerry was dismissive and somewhat bothered that I even called. In fact, he hung up on me.

I dialed right back and read him the riot act. I told him his aunt had always been there for him and he should at least talk to her. He just said, "Uh huh," and hung up again. I called him back a third time and told him he was a piece of crap, but he cut me off.

Aunt Kathy made it through the surgery. I never told her about the responses I had gotten from Uncle Dan, Pastor Keith, or her precious Jerry. She reached out to everyone, to notify them she was ok and would make a speedy recovery. They acted like everything was normal.

For a short time after the operation, Aunt Kathy was a new person. I might even say she was human. She was giddy, and even remorseful at times. Out of

guilt, Aunt Kathy wanted to give me money for tend-
ing to her through her ordeal. I kept telling her that
she owed me nothing. She was persistent, so I said I
would accept the money only if she called it a loan. It
was weird, because I didn't need it; but to soothe her,
I took the loan and paid her back three months later.

The experience of caring for her changed me, too.
I had little faith in her survival, but I'd watched that
old Christian pray, and I'd pray when hope was bleak.
Not only had I witnessed her prayers being answered,
I was genuinely there in mind and in spirit.

PART VIII:
HOUSTON, WE HAVE A PROBLEM

Here Comes the Light

"Whoa, Dude! You're telling me that all that praying finally worked out for mean old Aunt Kathy?" Dylan asked.

I laughed. "Yeah, well, it appears so. She came through her surgery with flying colors and outlived most of her siblings."

He scratched his head. "You sure had some bat shit crazy ladies in your life."

"Oh man, don't even get me started!"

Dylan motioned for the bartender and ordered another round. This guy could drink Frank Sinatra himself under the table. He had lapped me a few times, but I kept a steady pace.

When the drinks arrived, he said, "Hey, did you ever find that last guy you were looking for after the blast over in Afghanistan?"

"We did, but he was hurt real bad."

I picked up the story where I had left off.

Our camp had been a fortress of three reinforced concrete and dirt walls that stood ten feet tall, with a ten by ten foot iron gate. That barrier was a buffer to anything outside of camp. It would have taken a steel train just to breach it.

The bomb had been placed in an 18-wheeler that was parked by the gym. Its blast tore through the walls like an eraser to drawing paper. The iron gate was blown completely out of sight.

Me, Hayward, and the gang received information that Derrick was buried beneath the rubble of the gym. We headed over to where the building used to be. The structure had been completely leveled in the blast. It was nothing more than a pile of wood, sheet metal, and rocks. Derrick was somewhere underneath all that wreckage. We had to work quickly.

We hammered away at the sheet metal, but it quickly became obvious we were fighting a losing battle. There was no way we would reach him in time with the tools we had on hand. We desperately needed some heavy machinery. Arrangements were made for a crane, but we had no idea how long it would take to arrive.

Time crept onward. The cold brought on a thick fog and frost settled over the camp. Our doubts were stronger than our hope. Privately, I wasn't sure if Derrick would make it.

Suddenly, men bearing bright lights and automatic weapons appeared in the open hole where the gate used to be. This had to be the Taliban's final push. As the approaching lights blinded us, I looked for cover and said a prayer. There was nowhere to hide.

As the men got closer, two cranes rolled into camp on their heels. This had to be a death sandwich. I felt paralyzed, like in a nightmare. If these guys were shooting, we were certainly easy pickings. I asked for God to make it quick.

Unbeknownst to us, Ty, a supervisor and liaison to the military, had taken over all of the coordination for the rebuild and rescue operation. He had cleared the way for the Quick Reaction Force (QRF) and cranes to come inside the camp. It was not the Taliban; it was our own military! I wish I had known Ty was behind the scenes, because I went beyond "touching cotton". Sad and embarrassed, this wasn't the time or place to change my underwear. I stood frozen like a kid at a parade.

The QRF/Marines combed the grounds for terrorists and potential threats. One of the female soldiers had two different colored eyes and reminded me of Dead Eye Red. She was an omen of hope. The cranes bellowed in with a thundering roar and immediately began removing the debris on top of Derrick. What would have taken hours of our time and effort was accomplished in a matter of minutes. Derrick was freed and still alive, but he had to be evacuated out of Afghanistan with haste. He was dehydrated and had some internal injuries, but ultimately, he made it. We all did.

Dylan was still clutching his cocktail. "Jesus, man. What an ordeal! I can't believe you all lived to tell the tale."

"Yeah, it took many days to regroup after the explosion, but miraculously, we did all survive."

"Dude, talk about explosions! What about that night you spent in jail? Your wife had your daughter call the cops on you? What the hell happened with her? Did you finally find your groove in Memphis?"

Ahhh, this was a switch. For the first time all day, Dylan was more curious about my life on the home-front than the blast in Afghanistan.

"Let me tell you, Dylan. Things didn't exactly improve right away. There was a target on my back at work and at home. Out-running the bullets was practically impossible. I'll tell you all about it." And back in time again we went.

I Be Dog Gone

Loathe and envy don't take time off. Even though I had made tremendous inroads at Memphis Center, the naysayers and idiots were still not pleased I was among them. After fourteen years on the job, my detractors started a campaign to have me removed.

My offenses were:

#1: I bought a brand new candy apple red Corvette. My coworkers didn't like seeing me driving a flashy sports car. We all made the same amount of money, but they chose to buy big homes. The Corvette was my fantasy and it was by far the best thing I ever bought for myself.

#2: After watching the Lakers beat the Celtics, I was approached by one of the Controllers. He got up in my face with a sneer and said, "Not all Celtics fans are in Boston!" I stepped aside and responded, "Good for you!"

The Controller became even more hostile and flung out a stinging insult. "You FNG!" As I recalled from my big interview with the FAA years earlier, FNG meant "Freaking Nigger." I snatched the guy and pinned him up against the wall. Luckily for him, some people standing nearby stepped in to separate us.

We were both escorted to the boss's office for corrective action.

After talking with the boss and the witnesses, I was cleared of any transgressions. I apologized and explained I thought "FNG" was a racial slur, like "eeny meeny miny moe," (which had recently been a big story in the news after a schoolteacher attached the nursery rhyme to the refrain "catch a nigger by the toe"). The boss assured me that "FNG" was a military acronym that meant "Freaking New Guy." Okay, so I had been misinformed. My bad. But I was far from new, so the explanation didn't add up.

The boss left the Controller and me alone to talk things over. I wanted to be a man about what happened, so I asked for his forgiveness and offered to buy him a drink after work.

The Controller looked me square in the eyes, and said, "A drink won't be necessary. I said what I meant the first time. Eeny meeny miny moe!" And with that, he walked out of the room.

Maybe I deserved it for putting my hands on him. Either way, he delivered the hardest blow without even raising a finger.

As volatile as the incident with the Controller had been, it turned out the worst of my misdeeds was rooting against the Kentucky Wildcats. It may sound petty, but in the South, college sports are everything. People go absolutely nuts over them.

My female supervisor, who was very well liked and had unlimited power, was a huge Kentucky

Wildcats super fan. So was her husband, who had even bigger connections than she did. When they found out I was pulling for my alma mater, Mississippi State University, to beat the Wildcats, they started a scheme to keep me from certifying for a transfer I had requested. They tried to prove I couldn't meet the standards necessary for the new role, and attempted to have me removed from the facility. I thought it was a stupid prank gone bad, but the joke was squarely on me.

The situation got so out of hand, I had to file a grievance with the FAA in Memphis over the way I was treated. The FAA is a government civil service organization like the IRS, the Post Office, or the FBI. All agencies of the government have an in-house process to validate or dismiss grievances. Even though I knew the agents who review cases usually side with the government, filing a grievance was my only angle to save my job. It was the Hail Mary to beat all Hail Marys.

In the eleventh hour, another coworker exposed the conspiracy and saved my career. Although I was thrilled to be reinstated with the FAA, I had zero level of comfort or confidence about staying at Memphis Center. Even after all those years of earning my way, I could still be destroyed at any time for anything. The people in that place wanted a puppet-on-a-string or a punching bag. That was not me.

I felt too insecure and paranoid to stick around Memphis. Plus, things had gone even further south with my daughter's mother. I was depressed and lonely, and needed a change. The first chance I got, I left for greener pastures in Houston, Texas. Go *Bulldogs, dammit.*

Dead Man Walking

When I left the Memphis Air Traffic Control Center in 2000 for Houston, Texas, I had no idea my troubles would beat me to my new job. Air traffic control is a small world. Most Controllers either know each other or know someone who knows something about you. When you have a fallout with vindictive co-workers at one facility, they find a way to poison the environment at your next location. This is exactly what happened in my case.

The scoundrels who wanted me out at Memphis Center had connections in Houston. My "reputation" as a troublemaker preceded me. The outright racial discrimination continued, and even though I cannot prove it, I'm sure the problems I faced in Houston were an extension from my time in Memphis. I tried to fight like a beast from yonder, but I was a lone soldier in that war.

After five years of dodging bullets, I was finally forced to file a second grievance with the FAA. During the Equal Employment Opportunity Commission (EEOC) proceedings, I was able to expose countless lies, falsified documents, faulty procedures, neglected protocols, and double standards levied at me by managers, supervisors, and co-workers.

Even though I won nearly every argument while proving I was the only one targeted, the judge ruled she could not find any patterns of discrimination. With that decision, I was forced out of my position in Houston through a naked and obvious reprisal. The FAA had won and a sound message had been sent, with me as the example. I was a dead man walking.

A Hard Loss

While I was trying to navigate the bloody battlefield of the Houston Air Traffic Control Center, I got a call from my dad. It was the spring of 2003, and it had been five years since we'd last spoken. He said he wanted to see me, but he was a twelve-hour drive away. I had my hands full at work, so I told him I'd visit for Thanksgiving.

I didn't make it in time. Dad passed away that October. We never got to have our talk.

I got my family together to attend Dad's funeral. I was still bitter about the way he'd treated me when my daughter was born, but it was time for closure and respect. I gathered my strength as the day of his service drew near, but irony breaks suckers every day.

At his memorial, I was the emotional bastard who couldn't get it together. As tough as I tried to be, I couldn't fight back my tears. All the things we had lost or never done came bubbling out. We never went fishing. We never went on a road trip. We never had a beer. We never went to a game. The list was far too long. Beyond the empty vacuum of, "What if..." and "If only..." I had lost his calming force and his voice of reason forever. It was a hard loss, during a very hard time.

Turn Me On

Within ten days of my dismissal from Houston Air Traffic Control, I got a heads up from a coworker that Monroe, Louisiana was badly in need of Controllers. I drove through the night for an impromptu interview.

During our meeting, I was able to convince the Monroe manager, Albert Ogelsby, to demand the FAA keep me employed so that he could hire me at his facility. Mere days before Houston Center put me on the streets, Mr. Ogelsby did what he had to do. I landed the position and was able to get out of dodge for another fresh start. In December of 2006, I made the move from Houston to Monroe, Louisiana.

Albert Ogelsby and I were quite the odd couple. He was a deeply Southern white guy, chiseled straight out of Louisiana folklore. He had a big love for country music, hunting, and fishing, and was a down to earth, good-hearted man. I was a straight-laced African American, attuned to big city life. I was liberal-minded and wild about jazz, pop, and R&B music.

Luckily, Mr. Ogelsby was a good judge of character, and cared more about hard work than the color of someone's skin or petty rumors. He put his trust in me despite the garbage my detractors tried to peddle.

As I advanced in my new position, Mr. Ogelsby sent me to the Federal Aviation Academy in Oklahoma City, for a skills-enhancement class. I'd been to the Academy before, but never in my wildest dreams did I imagine going back. A lot had changed. I was learning about a new field within Air Traffic Control that required a different skillset. After fourteen years as a Controller, I was now part of the up and coming newbies. The classes were smaller. Even the jokes were different.

Our class had a female instructor who taught us how to sequence airplanes for landing. In the middle of her demonstration, she told us a common pilot request was a "hard turn to final," which was a sharp turn to line up to the airport. She told us she once told a pilot, "I have a hard turn on for you! How about imagining me in a dark room with black panties on?!" *Whoa!*

I never gave or received erotic instructions at the Academy, but I had fun learning new techniques in Oklahoma City.

An Opossum is Still a Possum

I had not seen my kids since I left Houston in 2006. Their mother and I were going through a divorce and they stayed at home with her. Since then, my nineteen-year-old daughter and I hit a rough patch. Unfairly, I blamed her for my unplanned marriage and the sacrifices I'd made. In some way, I thought she was responsible for the failure of the union. It was a dark time. My job was blowing up and my marriage was on the skids. My relationship with my kids took a major hit.

In Oklahoma, the hands of God brought us back together. My daughter was attending college in Kansas, which was only a three-hour drive. She was on the basketball team at school. Even though I taught her many of her on-court moves, I hadn't seen her play in years. Due to our newfound proximity and the rebirth of my career, I could go see her games and be like the other fathers in the stands. According to my daughter, I was the loudest dad in the crowd.

Seeing her again inspired me to bring my son to town for a family reunion. He was seven years old at the time. The three of us stayed at the Great Wolf Lodge and Water Park. I spent most of our first night hugging the life out of my kids. I remember my son said, "Dad, you're smushing me!" I couldn't help it. I was over the moon to be with them.

It was amazing to feel like a hands-on dad again. I gave my son his first boxing and wrestling lesson and he was all smiles. My daughter caught me up on her new jokes. She said she hated opossums and I said, "Ok, I'll bite. Go ahead and tell me why."

"Well, not only do opossums try to play dead, but they also try to trick you with the way they spell their name. You know it's O-p-o-s-s-u-m-s, and not Possums!"

Suddenly, my son burst into the room and said he'd been shoved down by one of the bigger kids at the park. As any parent would, I asked why the other boy pushed him. My son admitted it was because he wouldn't let the boy's sister onto the water slide.

I admonished him for not being a gentleman to the little girl, but then I challenged his toughness. I asked him what happened to all the great boxing and wrestling moves I'd shown him the night before. With tears streaming down his face, my son gave an emotional response. He said, "Dad, that boy could have taken me out in one shot." Needless to say, I blame my own mentoring. We had a recap in self-defense before he went back to Houston. I looped the opossum strategy into the mix. You can be down but not dead, as I'd learned a few times around the old block.

Carey, Take Me Away!

Leaving Houston was a good move from a job security standpoint, but a very bad move for my wallet. I lost a massive chunk of my salary. To make matters worse, I was in the middle of a divorce. I could no longer afford the life I had prior to my termination. The FAA has strict guidelines regarding financial responsibility, so filing for Chapter 7 or 11 would have caused me to lose the bronze medal job I'd fought so hard for.

The whole time I was in Louisiana, from 2006 until 2009, I was waiting and hoping to get a position with Quality Air Traffic Control. Quality ATC was a contracting position with a much higher salary than I was making back in Houston, and considerably more than I was making in Monroe.

While I waited and held out for the new opportunity, I lived as meagerly as I could to stave off bankruptcy. For three years, my home was a broken down Recreational Vehicle with no running water, no air conditioning, no television, no toilet, no shower, and no Internet. It was a total throwback to my boyhood years as a scrapper. I'd tasted the sweet life in Memphis and Houston, but I was no stranger to the streets and knew how to find what I needed. No doubt, I existed in the shadowy depths of Monroe, Louisiana.

Each day, I got up and headed to one of a handful of hotels for a birdbath in the restroom. After work, I sought out happy hour specials to overload on free chicken wings, cheese plates, or tacos. The free appetizers were dinners to me in those days. Most of the people who worked at the hotels saw me so often they thought I was a Diamond Member, and I made a lot of friends at those establishments.

Finally, in November 2009, I got a call from Quality Air Traffic Control. The placement officer, Carey Lambert, assured me he would bring me onboard as an international contractor. He mentioned Afghanistan as a likely assignment. When I first interviewed for the job, I sold Quality ATC not only on my skills and experience but on my good health and willingness to travel. I had been waiting for a new beginning ever since I left Houston. Quality ATC was my big break into a new endeavor and I jumped on the opportunity. When the placement officer called, I said, "Carey, take me away! I'll go anywhere!"

Going to work in a country at war didn't bother me. I had a keen awareness for picking up on trouble and things out of the ordinary. That inner radar had been my protection from hostile entities for as long as I could remember. I figured it would serve me well over in Afghanistan, too.

Accepting the job with Quality ATC was a huge relief. The salary boost felt like financial redemption. My ex-wife had gotten remarried and moved thousands of miles away. Though my child support was always on time, I didn't have the freedom to make frequent visits because I worked six days a week. Plus, my rat-infested trailer was no place for my young son or college-aged daughter. Quality ATC gave me both the means and the freedom to see them more often. Now, I could be more involved in their lives.

I took the job and my whole world changed. There was no looking back, and there was plenty to leave behind: racism, continued weird family dynamics, monetary struggles, my broken marriage. It was all in the rearview mirror now.

PART IX:
OFF TO OTHER WARS

Inside the Wire

I picked up the thread of the blast story and told Dylan how back in Kabul, Ty worked the phones like a NASA Controller. He was in full operations mode, to get his people to safety. Ty decided, enough Safety Room triage; we had to relocate. The threat of a follow up attack was imminent and we were still without power. Ty instructed us to prepare to leave the barracks. We were bussed over to the military base and assigned temporary bunks.

Our worksite was very near to our camp and the base, which we visited practically every day for food, haircuts, shopping, business, mail, or recreation. There was a coalition of forces from around the world at that post. Our camp was considered Outside the Wire and the military base was Inside the Wire. It was definitely safer Inside the Wire because of the scrutiny, the security, and the soldiers with guns. However, being Outside the Wire allowed more freedoms and less constraint due to military procedures.

I knew a lot of the servicemen at the military base, but after the bombing it was like being at a funeral. There wasn't a lot of talking; just a few hugs and a few tears among friends. For the first time as an independent contractor, I felt like a battered soldier. Although my experience was only a small taste of what some servicemen go through, our soldiers and military personnel will always have my deepest respect.

Dylan started prodding me like a detective. "Let's go back to that outside the fence thing."

"You mean, Outside the Wire? What about it?"

"How does that work?"

I explained, "It's basically a contractor or mercenary thing. People who are willing to accept the risks of the job want some of the comforts of home. So, these big contracting companies create camps with dorms that are hotel-like, with heavy protections for those daring workers. Most contractors preferred camp life Outside the Wire, even with the risks."

"So, you got to see some of the Afghani citizens."

"Yes, plenty of them." I told Dylan that I saw many things we Americans take for granted: people living without electricity, without internet, heating, air conditioning, restrooms, or drinking water. And yet, even though the people there are very poor, everyone has a cell phone.

"Hmm," he said. "It sounds rough, but it also sounds like the way you grew up. Not to mention, your living situation in Louisiana."

"True, their living conditions were indeed familiar to me."

"So tell me then, when did you decide to cut bait?"

"Every contractor who has ever done more than one tour has asked himself, 'What in the world am I doing?' I was in the belly of Afghanistan and it spat me out like it had so many before. After a few days Inside the Wire, when my nerves had calmed, I made the decision to leave what had become hell on earth. I had to get away from the bloody, terrifying scene. That's when I decided to buy a one-way ticket to Thailand, to soak away all these memories of that wretched explosion.

"Now, here we are. On an empty beach in the middle of nowhere, and you have forced me to dredge it all up again."

Dylan passed me a double shot of rum. He could tell this wasn't easy for me; he sensed my struggle. With a grin, he said, "I don't know about *forced*, but no doubt this has been a deep dredge."

I said, "Dylan, you may need that drink. Let me take this sad tale home." He'd been a good audience, and my stories had taken an unexpected toll on me. Methodically, I had bitten my lip to hold back swelling emotion. No doubt the end had come, and all dead ends lead back to Jerry and Mom.

Paradise Lost

My uncle Dan passed away in 2012, from a failed heart operation. When Uncle Dan was six feet under, Aunt Kathy inherited his estate right from under his six daughters, just as it had been plotted. Mom and I hoped Aunt Kathy would do the right thing and return Uncle Dan's property to his girls. It was one of the few times Mom and I were on the same page.

True to character, Aunt Kathy would have nothing to do with our suggestions. The rebirth of humanity she experienced after her quintuple bypass had faded almost as quickly as it occurred. She was back to her mean old self, planning to gift her brother's estate solely to Jerry. Everyone went into an uproar over that information.

Mom entered full meltdown mode and ranted about Aunt Kathy being possessed by dead dogs, ghosts, haints, and evil spirits. She had episode after episode, all in regard to Aunt Kathy's intentions. No one was looking out for Uncle Dan's daughters, and Mom's protective instincts fueled a desire for decency to prevail. She pleaded nonstop: "Sister, what are you doing? Sister, don't allow those dogs to get into your head! This is the work of the evil spirits!"

But it wasn't enough. Mom had no power, and neither did I. Aunt Kathy brushed Mom off and said, "Those girls don't deserve Dan's house. Nah, Nah, Nah. Dan left it to me, and I'm giving it to the best one of all!"

In a truly terrible act of malice, Jerry got the keys to the castle that should have been his cousins' inheritance. Aunt Kathy had humiliated me before, but this kind of stink can sever families forever. Even though I had nothing to do with Aunt Kathy's decision, my relatives viewed me as the enemy as well.

On the day of the exchange, I attempted one final effort to get Jerry to sign the property over to its rightful heirs. He was drunk and belligerent, and having none of it. He even accused me of trying to steal his stuff. "...as you always have," he said. Then he added, "But not this time, buddy boy. It's about time y'all recognize who I am."

Jerry was so inebriated when he delivered his little speech that he had to brace himself to stand upright. Throughout the spectacle, Aunt Kathy was all smiles. She was actually glowing. It was as if she had planned this all along.

Jerry also got Uncle Dan's Ford SUV and iPhone. The three houses, however, were not entirely free. Jerry would have to pay the estate taxes on all of them, which the cousins had been paying even after Aunt Kathy assumed the deeds. This level of responsibility was way too much for Jerry to handle, as time would reveal.

Immediately after he left the attorney's office from signing the paperwork, Jerry got a speeding ticket in his new SUV. He literally drove off the lot like a wanted fugitive. Being that he was drunk, he really was a danger to society. No doubt, he should have been detained, but Jerry was always as slippery as a greased pig. No one dared to stop him.

Unfortunately, Jerry had far more stupidity in his blood than he had luck. He lost his iPhone in a card game of Spades. He pleaded with the new owner to let him use the phone to call someone for more money, to stay in the game. That guy was no dummy; he charged Jerry a service fee to use the phone, and Jerry wound up walking away from the game with a bill that was double the value of the mobile device he had lost.

Jerry wasn't bashful about showing off his Ford SUV. If I knew anything about my brother, I knew his chariot would not last long. He told me I was not to be seen anywhere near his vehicle, and if I needed a ride, I better have some money to pay for gas. All I could say was, "Ok, Cowboy," and then wait for the inevitable.

About two weeks later, he called to ask me for a couple of bucks for gas. I laughed and took the opportunity to remind him I was to go nowhere near his vehicle. Jerry said, "I still want you to stay away from my truck. You'll get your damn money back after I get it started!" This logic didn't add up, but I agreed to give him some gas money. He instructed me to bring it by the house, but when I got there, both he and the truck were gone. I used the key under the front door mat and left the money on the kitchen table, knowing I'd never see it again.

Days later, I heard that Jerry had lost his truck to a pawnshop dealer. Apparently, he was using the truck's title to fund his drug dealing business, which was a piss poor operation. He smoked far more ganja than he sold and couldn't afford to reclaim the truck.

Jerry's downward spiral didn't end there. The houses he inherited from Uncle Dan were in need of repairs, but he never attempted any upgrades. He also neglected to pay the taxes, as predicted. I saw where the situation was headed and offered to buy the buildings. My plan was to work a deal for my cousins to get back what was rightfully theirs from the beginning. But Jerry rejected my offer with a firm "No" followed by a "Hell, no!"

Tragically, the houses were condemned and taken by the county. I told Jerry he should have allowed me to keep the property in the family. His response was, "You have enough of our stuff." Once again, I was floored by his comment, but Jerry somehow felt he had to play 'keep away' with me. I have to say, he played that game the way he played his life, ruled by fool's logic.

The Walls Stand Silent Now

Dylan let out a deep sigh. "Man, you walked a goat rope. The bombing, the women, your brothers, your mother, your aunt, the bullies, all those jobs."

I let out a deep sigh too. "Indeed, I did."

Out of nowhere, he asked whatever happened to Mom. With tears in my eyes, I relayed, "Dylan, that may be the deepest gaping hole of them all."

You see, Mom passed away in February of 2017. I was here, in Thailand, when I received an unexpected call. Mom had been sick for some time but no one told me. Not Mom herself, not Aunt Kathy, and not my brothers. Aunt Kathy had even persuaded Mom to accept her fate without proper medical attention. Of course, I was as angry as a bucking bull, but that wasn't going to bring her back. It was time to let go and let God have her.

I had to take a flight home from Thailand and face the family. There I was, back in Mississippi, trying to get the brothers together to pay Mom her final respects. Jerry was the toughest one to get on board. He wanted nothing to do with me. I had never treated him like the king he thought he was born to be, and he still had that liquid courage. He gassed up before coming to see me and reeked of alcohol like bad cologne.

Fully fortified, he told me I'd broken protocol my whole life. "You bought Carl stuff without doing things the proper way."

I was lost. "What are you talking about?"

"I'm Jerry. That stuff was supposed to go through me first!"

"Really?"

"Yeah, really. You never knew how to do stuff right. You looked out for Mom's boyfriends when you should have come my way."

"Oh, I see. I was supposed to alert you to my personal transactions before giving anything to someone else?"

Jerry looked at me with his small, piercing, bloodshot eyes and calmly said, "Damn right!"

"HA!" Then, I left it at that. There was no reasoning with him.

At that point, I wasn't sure Jerry would make it to the funeral. He was determined to stick it to me any way he could, even if it meant not showing up for Mom's service. I was already heart-stricken, so I prepared to be unsurprised by whatever Jerry decided to do.

Everything around Mom's life had always been erratic and unpredictable; her ceremony was no different. As Pastor Keith delivered the eulogy, I thought of his sermon from Matthew 8:23-27. I wanted to hear him say, "Jesus calms the storm!" one last time.

In that same church where I had grown up, I began to reminisce over Mom's biggest and boldest stunts. Many of them had taken place right where I was sitting. I saw her hooting and hollering through the pews, causing a ruckus, riding her bicycle in the middle of the street to purposely hold up traffic; carrying a sheer umbrella that did nothing to shut out the sun on her way to church; doing donuts at the bus stop; chasing kids on her bicycle; crossing the road to deliberately force people off the sidewalk; and going nose to nose with "The Wall". Memories of her will dance in my head until my own time comes to an end.

I sat in the front row and wiped away my tears. I was shaking like a feather with my mind spinning out of control. Suddenly, Jerry, who had decided to grace us with his presence after all, raised his fist as if to say, "Charge!" I was shocked by his hand gesture. I didn't know if it was his way of getting everyone to notice he was in the house, or what. Then I got it. Jerry's raised fist was a tribute to Mom's battle with her demons.

I know Mom will continue to fight those ghosts, devils, dead dogs, and haints with all her fury. But from here on she won't have the world to distract her or slow her down. For once, my brother Jerry had done right by Mom. I thought to myself, "Do your thing, Mom. Charge! And give 'em Hell! I will love you forever."

Despite all our hardships, saying goodbye to Mom will never seem appropriate. Deep down, I know she will never leave me. Deep down I know her demons still own me.

The End.

EPILOGUE—The Devil's Doorstep

Dylan and I sat quietly after I shared the news of Mom's death. It was a hard one to swallow for sure, and still pretty raw for me.

Eventually, my companion stirred. He sat up and said, "I have been with you from story to story. I have heard your moments of death and destruction. We have drunk ourselves from intoxication to sobriety, then back to drunk again."

"This is true."

He was empathetic but restless. Then, Dylan pulled out the million-dollar question. "So, what are you going to do now? Will you stay here with the ladies and the liquor?"

"I knew this question was coming, but I'm not sure you're going to like my answer. I've only just now figured it out myself."

"I would never judge you, my friend."

I suddenly felt relief, and a bond. This very long, soul searching day with Dylan had been great therapy for me. I had bared my personal history to him and he had become a friend, better than any other friend I'd had in my adulthood.

I hadn't yet fully examined all of the particulars, but during the course of my conversation with Dylan, I made the decision to go back to Quality ATC and

Afghanistan. It seemed to be my destiny more than the beaches of Thailand, even with its bikini-clad babes and bottomless cocktails. For my friend's benefit, I attempted to reconstruct the decision that would lead me back to the devil's doorstep.

"Dylan, I haven't been the same since the bombing. Honestly, who would be?"

He nodded in agreement, and I continued. Yes, I was given a new lease on life, but I felt as if I was living each day through a camera lens. When I lost Mom, something shifted. Somehow, her passing seemed like a gateway to my rebirth, but there were three key factors I still couldn't shake.

One: I watched every moving bicycle until it disappeared completely out of sight; waiting and waiting for the rider to perform a circus act or do something extraordinary like Mom would have done. I was so accustomed to her arrivals being outrageous and totally off the cuff, witnessing a bicycle rider acting normal became a letdown for me. It was eerily disappointing *not* to witness a cuckoo moment.

Two: Every Lisa, Lilly, or Elizabeth mentioned within earshot only made me hear Liza, Liza, and Liza. I became restless at any variation of Mom's name, like it was dejavu or Groundhog Day, again and again. I froze up out of habit from pure fear and utter shame. I was a lost white dove in a snowstorm.

Three: Losing Mom destroyed my inner balance. I was always on guard when she was around. Now, I am unattached, floating, drifting out to sea. Water is no longer wet and music has no sound. Her death removed many challenges but left no answers. I even found myself talking to The Wall, and thought, *There has to be something here that triggered Mom's demons.* But The Wall never talked back. It left me feeling empty, and stupid for trying. Maybe Mom took her demons with her after all.

I've realized that I need to be stimulated. I have to return to Afghanistan. The war, the poverty, the bombing make no sense, but it has been my world. My life before was nothing but a series of obstacles to overcome with jerks at every turn. I have faced death and survived, by the grace of God.

Dylan was more disturbed by this revelation than being drunk could buffer. He grabbed me for a long embrace during which he seemed to be trying to transfer a measure of sanity. Sadly, soundness of mind doesn't work that way. My mind was made up. I wasn't ready to accept getting older and sitting on a porch. I was addicted to the international lifestyle, and I didn't care for the politics of home.

As Dylan released me, he said, "God bless you, my man. I hope you're at peace with your decision."

I shook his hand and said, "Indeed, I am. Life just happens. It's never fair and nothing is promised. But life keeps coming at you from different angles, whether you're ready or not. The biggest thing you and I have in common is we have fewer tomorrows than we have yesterdays. And I'm going back to being a Controller who is in control of my tomorrows.

"Thank you for listening, my friend. I've shared every spoke of my life's wagon wheel with you on this beach, and you've helped me more than you can ever know."

With that, Dylan motioned to the bartender for the bill. He made good on his promise to pick up the tab, but it was me who was indebted.

Acknowledgements

I have to thank God for protecting me as I fought for my life in that mighty explosion. Without his mercy, I would not have been able to share my story of survival or the history that came before the blast.

I'd like to dedicate this book to the memory of my mom. Her passing was the final motivation I needed to share my stories.

I want to thank my dad, step-mom, my brother and sister, for being so accepting. You have all been awesome from day one. Honestly, I don't know how we did it but we did. I really love you all.

I have to thank Randy Ogles (Retired Air Traffic Manager at Monroe Tower, Monroe Louisiana) and Parry Campbell (Project Manager at Midwest ATC). You guys really employed me at a low moment in my life. No way can I measure what you guys did for me mentally and financially.

Thanks for taking a chance on me when no one else was willing to do so.

I'd like to thank John P. Dennis – motivational speaker, President of Georgia Writer's Museum, and author of *Men Raised by Women*, *The Straw Man*, and *The Blank Check* – for helping me develop this book.

I want to give a big thanks to Brooke White for the

reshaping and the impact she gave to my writing. It was Brooke's professionalism and wit that helped to narrow my scope to most of my stories.

I want to thank Lamont Ingram for his words, wit, and wisdom, and Joshua Shorter-Ivey for his encouragement and support to expose this book far and wide.

I want to honor the troops and the contractors who have lost their lives in Afghanistan. They shall never be forgotten.

About The Author

Harold Phifer was born and raised in Columbus, Mississippi. His first twenty-five years were spent entirely in his home state. After graduating Mississippi State and Jackson State Universities, he became a highly specialized air traffic controller, living and working as an international contractor, serving numerous tours in Iraq and Afghanistan. SURVIVING CHAOS is his second book.

Thank You for Reading

SURVIVING CHAOS:
How I Found Peace at a Beach Bar

If you enjoyed this book, please consider leaving
a short review on your website of choice.

Reviews help both readers and authors.
Posting a review for any book is an easy way
to support good writing and encourage
the release of quality content.

For the Latest from Rise & Read Free Press

Facebook: @rnrfreepress
Twitter: @rnrfreepress
Instagram: @rnrfreepress

rnrfreepress.com

Made in the USA
Monee, IL
03 March 2023

29120848R00174